No hiding place

Essays on the new nature and poetry

JOHN BARNIE

UNIVERSITY OF WALES PRESS
CARDIFF
1996

© John Barnie, 1996

British Library Cataloguing-in-Publication Data.
A catalogue record for this book is available from the British Library.

ISBN 0-7083-1342-6

Published with the financial support of the Arts Council of Wales

Cover design by Rhiain M. Davies, Cain, Carmarthen
Printed in Wales by Dinefwr Press, Llandybïe

Contents

I went to the rock
        to hide my face
The rock cried out –
        No hiding place.

        (*traditional*)

Acknowledgements

Some of these essays first appeared in *Planet*, while 'Poetry and the new nature' was first published in *Poetry Wales*. 'What do we mean by nature?', 'At the zoo', 'A walk along Corsons Inlet' and 'A personal history of reading' are previously unpublished.

Lyric extracts from the compositions of Robert Johnson © (1978) 1990, 1991 King of Spades Music. All rights reserved. Used by permission.

My thanks to Helle Michelsen for her criticism and to Ceinwen Jones of the University of Wales Press for her meticulous editing.

Om man frågor mig om mina litterära planer svarar jeg att de är egentligen detsamma som ideliga försök att kunna formulera någonting som kan tänkas vara centralt för civilisationen. Jag tror inte längre på några partier eller någon slags politisk frälsning för världen. I stället försöker jag i den mån jag kan genomtränga problemen, granska den moderna tillvaron utifrån aspekter som man skulle kunna kalla buddistiska. Min erfarenhet och åsikt är den att vi, mer än vi någonsin vill erkänna eller förmår överblicka, är teknikens fångar och därmed också ömsevis maskincivilisationens slavar eller dess förmenta herrar; två saker som jag, ifall man räknar på lång sikt, anser vara samma sak.

Harry Martinson, 'Var är vår häpenhet?'

If I'm asked about my literary plans, I reply that they amount to repeated attempts to formulate something which might be considered central to civilization. I no longer believe in parties or in any kind of political salvation for the world. Instead, I try as best I can to penetrate the problem, examine the modern condition, from a position which you might call Buddhist. It's my experience and opinion that, more than we will ever acknowledge, or be able to conceive, we are the prisoners of technology, and by the same token, either the slaves of machine-civilization or its putative masters; two things which, if looked at in the long term, I consider to be the same.

Harry Martinson, 'Where is our amazement?'

Introduction

The Wordsworthian view that poetry and human nature cannot be meaningfully divorced from the rest of nature seems to me axiomatic. However, nature is not the same as it was in Wordsworth's time. Between then and now stands the figure of Charles Darwin. His theory of evolution is a lens through which we now have to see nature and ourselves. Though perhaps 'learn to see' is a more accurate description. Nearly 140 years after the publication of *The Origin of Species*, most of us still only have a vague notion of Darwin's ideas and an even vaguer one of the new synthesis of evolutionary theory with genetics.

This is partly because the ideas of evolutionary biology are not easy to understand – in fact they are easy to misunderstand. But it is also because Darwin's theory is threatening. It realigns the human relation to nature in such radical ways that emotionally we are barely able to cope with it. We do not yet know how to incorporate this new perception of ourselves and the 3.5-billion-year history of life on Earth into our general culture in a meaningful way.

A few years ago when the Bank of England redesigned its banknotes, it was proposed that Darwin's portrait be used on the back of one as a suitably eminent Englishman. The proposal was rejected, however, on the grounds that his theory is still not generally accepted. Yet the theory of evolution has stood up to nearly a century and a half of intense and sometimes hostile investigation by scientists and is now universally accepted in the scientific community – that part of society best able to judge it.

1

Darwin was rejected because the cautious Bank of England did not want to cause offence. Of all the great Victorian thinkers, Darwin is the one whose ideas demand attention and also require, unless they can be disproved, that we reassess completely our understanding of what we are. For the evolutionary view of life is the final blow delivered by science to human self-importance in the universe, to our belief in the grounding of ethics in something other than ourselves, and to almost all other aspects of customary human belief.

American fundamentalists were quick to perceive this. It is not the new physics or the new cosmology that threatens Christianity. By means of a sleight of hand it is possible for liberal theologians and mystics to embrace particle physics and attempt to incorporate it into a new Christian model.

But liberal Christians are slower to take up the challenge of Darwinism which quietly undermines theology by making it superfluous to any explanation of how we came to be what we are. On the one or two occasions I have discussed this with Christian intellectuals, it has been clear how little they have bothered to find out about evolutionary biology which remains for the most part outside their frame of reference. A nod in the direction of Teilhard de Chardin's evolutionary speculations is not enough, for these have nothing to do with Darwinian evolution.

American fundamentalists must be given credit for recognizing the challenge of Darwinism to their beliefs, even if their attempt to confound it with 'Creation' science involves a parody of scientific method and is as groundless as Teilhard de Chardin's notion of the evolution of life towards an eventual mystical union with God.

Poets, like other individuals, can turn away from unpleasant truth, though with diminishing returns for their poetry. Since the Romantics we have been on an intellectual journey in which the mind seeks the truth whatever its consequences. As we probe deeper, the received truth of authority dwindles behind us. Truth is not something given but something to be sought by the unaccommodated mind. This is so for the poet as for the scientist, though with this difference: the poet's function is to celebrate truth, to find joy in it without which he or she cannot create.

It may seem ironic, therefore, that celebration in an obvious sense is more apparent in the writings of contemporary scientists such as Stephen Jay Gould, Richard Dawkins and Edward O. Wilson. Their delight in the intellectual challenge of their discipline and its history in geological deep time is boundless and communicates itself to the reader of their essays and books. Yet they only go so far, refusing for the most part to discuss the way in which its guiding ideas, seeping down, can seem oppressive, delivering us over to a world of diminished returns and diminished prospects.

Of the scientists just mentioned, Gould appears to evade the issue in his popular articles, merely observing that human meaning must be sought elsewhere than in nature, while Dawkins delights in a Huxley-like battering of the Christians with reason. Winning the intellectual battle seems to be enough for him. Only Wilson, as one of the founders of sociobiology, attempts a synthesis of the neo-Darwinist position with revised ideas about society and ethics. But Wilson is too much a product of his own rationality. People are motivated not so much by reason as by feeling. It is how they *feel* about themselves and their world that matters to them most. The new world of the sociobiologists, as Wilson seems at times reluctantly to admit, will never come about because it is founded on reason alone and assumes that we will review our place in the biological scheme of things in a rational way.

But we cannot because feeling constantly breaks through, threatening to overwhelm us with despair. For our feelings are the deepest, oldest, most primitive and most finely tuned aspect of us as human animals. And here lies the problem. We feel rather than think our lives, but in the West we have for a long time structured feeling on the value-laden Christian under-standing of ourselves as part of, yet apart from, a nature that is under God's providence. That structure has been shattered by neo-Darwinism and we have at present nothing to put in its place.

Scientists are probably right not to focus publicly on this crisis of meaning. They are natural philosophers in the old sense, and their job is to come as close as possible to the truth about nature. They are not responsible for the consequences of this truth for our self-perception. When they do attempt to integrate moral

philosophy in a scientific structure, as Edward O. Wilson does in
On Human Nature, the result is often far from convincing.

For the poets it is different. Feeling is their sphere. They are
not philosophers, nor even for the most part systematic thinkers.
They intuit their thoughts, feel them with a great intensity and
make them felt in the minds of others who read their poems.
Because of this, poets have always held an ambiguous place in
society, both central and peripheral, respected and at times
dismissed, especially when they touch a collective wound.

In *No Hiding Place* I have for this reason set essays on nature
side by side with essays on poetry and poets, for poets express
the wound that science has dealt us in a way that the scientists
cannot do themselves.

Harry Martinson is a nature poet in the Wordsworthian sense:
in his extensive writings close observation of nature is integrated
in a philosophy of nature which includes the human. That
philosophy takes as its starting-point the ideas of evolutionary
biology. But Martinson also had a religious sensibility which
expressed itself in a secular form. Christianity is largely ignored
in his work, and, though he believed that our relationship to
nature is of the greatest importance, he was not a pantheist or a
nature mystic. That is to say, he did not believe that nature was
the door to any kind of mystical experience. Words such as 'God'
and 'soul' are used entirely, I think, in a metaphorical way,
transposing something of their transcendental meaning onto the
world of nature, without suggesting that there is anything
beyond it and the lives that we know.

This is central to his great space epic *Aniara*. We only have the
Earth and if we pollute and degrade it, we degrade ourselves.
The sun is presented in *Aniara* and elsewhere as a symbol of love,
though again not as a transcendent symbol. The Earth could be
transformed if we responded to it. It would not prevent the ice
sheets from engulfing Scandinavia again when the next ice age
comes, and it would not prevent the eventual extinction of our
species. But we are here, and here is not only all we have, it is
essentially good. That is what the human remnant on Aniara
comes to realize too late.

Love, however, is opposed by human destructiveness and evil.
Harry Martinson's views became more and more pessimistic
during the Second World War and the succeeding Cold War. He

became a sharp critic of the pace and nature of technological development in the West and the mass culture it created. For it led to the death of the spirit (in his secular sense) and the triumph of a materialist culture over love. He foresaw the despoiling of nature as a consequence.

Martinson became increasingly a Cassandra-like figure (a favourite reference of his in later years) in the materialist and prosperous Sweden of the 1950s and 1960s. He was inevitably shouted down as a reactionary. In much of this he resembles R. S. Thomas, though there is a greater generosity of spirit in Harry Martinson's works. But they separate over the ultimate meaning of nature. R. S. Thomas is of course familiar with evolutionary biology. He confronts its implications occasionally in the later poems, though with horror.

R. S. Thomas too is a Wordsworthian in his commitment to the parallel exploration of nature and human nature, but within a more traditional frame of reference than Martinson. For Thomas backs away from internalizing the implications of Darwinism. He has referred to himself as a nature mystic and although nature is there of and for itself in the poems, it always offers the prospect of a revelation or intimation of the transcendental, as in 'The Moor'. For this reason the new physics is more congenial to R. S. Thomas than neo-Darwinism. Unlike the latter, and following commentators like Fritjof Capra, the new physics appears not to close the door on God in the Christian sense.

Yet the transcendental in Thomas's poems seems at best deeply ambiguous, centred on the contemplation of an untenanted cross and a God who remains silent in the face of his creatures' anguish. The poems are far less Christian than some of their commentators claim. R. S. Thomas is more like a man sheltering in the porch of a dubious faith, looking out across a bleak terrain.

But he, like Harry Martinson, has been an early critic of our commitment to technology in a mass society, and of the shallowness and aimlessness of its drives. R. S. Thomas too is a modern Cassandra whose fate it is to tell the truth and be ignored.

A. R. Ammons is little known here, but he is an important post-war American poet, winner of the Bollingen Prize and author of twenty-one collections of poems. His approach to nature most resembles that of Martinson, but Ammons has a scientist's eye for forms and motions underlying nature which exist in a continuum that is constantly changing in its resonances and alliances. The human mind, in Ammons's poems, is a mirror image of this. It is possible, therefore, for us to perceive as in a mirror the truth of nature so long as we realize that each position on the continuum, each perception, is open to adjustment. Truth for us has to be provisional because of what we are and what nature is. There may be a more unifying truth or truths, but we may never be able to come at them. In Ammons's poems, such as in 'Corsons Inlet' discussed here, a new engagement with life as something provisional and open-ended demands an open attentiveness in the human mind, not Western culture's insistence on a closed, static world of absolute categories.

Robert Johnson is a different kind of poet from Martinson, Thomas and Ammons. A Mississippi bluesman murdered at the age of twenty-seven, he would not have been familiar with the ideas in this book. None the less he belongs here as a Romantic in a post-Darwinian world. In his songs, as in the poems of Martinson and Thomas, the journey is a powerful, recurring symbol. It is there too in the religious music of the South with which Johnson would have been familiar, but there the journey – and the destination at Heaven's gate – are foreknown. Johnson's journey is different, more like an attempted escape and fuelled by an inner desperation. It is the intense emotional equivalent of the intellectual journey of the Romantics. If Robert Johnson is reminiscent of another poet, it is not so much fellow bluesmen as Sylvia Plath. There is the same sense of shock, and after-shock, on listening to or reading their poems: the sense of someone whose life is driven to the extremes in the production of their art.

The essay on Robert Johnson is included here for this reason. Johnson is not a nature poet in the sense that R. S. Thomas and Harry Martinson are nature poets, but he shares with them a sensibility at the edge – the only place now where I believe it is possible to live an authentic life. The edge, the outer limit, may be philosophical, a matter of sensibility, as in the case of Thomas and Martinson, or it may be one of rending emotion as it is with Johnson. The connection between these very different poets is intuitive, not logical. But Johnson is a poet, like the others discussed here, who could only have been produced by our times. I can think of no one with a comparable sensibility in the pre-Romantic period.

To write as a non-specialist about the new nature is to invite criticism. I began reading about evolutionary biology because I wanted to know more. My early attraction to nature was entirely intuitive as I explored the hills and meadows and rivers around Abergavenny when I was a boy. Then, walking through the wood on the Little Skirrid, it was enough to watch a green woodpecker drumming high on the trunk of a tree, or a raven performing its acrobatic courtship flight. Everything was new.

It is a common experience, of course. So is growing up to see what you valued eroded and destroyed. Eventually I needed a broader perspective. I could not go out and watch birds with pleasure any longer. The shadow of what we are doing to the Earth fell across my enjoyment.

Reading *The Origin of Species* led me to books on the neo-Darwinian synthesis, but I also found myself turning to palaeontology and palaeoanthropology to try to understand the history of our genus in the geological record, as well as to socio-biology in an attempt to understand what we are and to place our destructiveness as a species in a broader historical context – historical, that is, in the sense of the 3.5-billion year history of nature.

These essays are the result of that reading. Written over the past five or six years, many of them for serial publication, they are not presented here as a single coherent thesis, but as reports from what seems to me the most significant intellectual adventure of our age. I must inevitably have over-simplified complex arguments in the process and unknowingly made mistakes of interpretation that will seem embarrassing to the specialist.

Yet the attempt to understand the results of other disciplines seems essential. Not only because the fragmentation of knowledge threatens to turn us all into narrow specialists, isolated intellectually from each other, but because, now more than ever in our species' history, it is important that we try to come to terms with what we are, what nature is, and our place in it.

At the same time we must listen to the poets whose poems are, in Harry Martinson's words,

> människosjälens lek med språkens själ
> och visionärens lek med ve och väl.
>
> the human soul's play with the soul of language
> and the visionary's play with sorrow and joy.

Through them we must learn to redirect our feelings that are frustrated and checked at every turn by the culture of mass society, learn how to turn the sun into 'kärlekens stjärna', the star of love.

What do we mean by nature?

When we use the word 'nature' we rarely stop to think what we mean by it, or to consider whether we might be misunderstood in conversation. General agreement is assumed even though 'nature' embraces a hugely complex, and for our purposes on Earth, practically all-embracing concept.

One reason is that most of us, most of the time, use it in a very loose way that *is* easily understood. Nature is simply the 'countryside' and all non-human things in it. Some might quibble, suggesting that the countryside is too deeply compromised by human use to mean nature in its true sense. Nature is 'wilderness', or what small fragments and refuges pass for wilderness in most of Europe. A fashionable twist on this, displacing 'nature' and 'countryside' on the lips of many is the 'environment'. Nature is the environment.

This word in this particular context had its origins in science, but it has passed into popular use in a debased form. To talk of the 'environment' rather than 'nature' is to establish credentials; it gives conversation a hard edge of science, though in practice this is rarely more than a veneer. It goes with an acquaintance with the problems of global warming and acid rain. The term still has a proper function in science, but when most of us use it we still mean little more than the countryside. Its greater level of abstraction is an indicator of urban culture's growing alienation from nature.

In general use the 'environment' is a cant word with an unfortunate undertow of meaning. For by definition an environment is something which surrounds a centre. Everywhere we turn, the 'environment' is; and we by extension are its centre. The term is homocentric and suits machine-civilization's view of things. But it is based on a wrong perspective, as is the related and equally misguided notion of 'stewardship'. Seen on the scale of geological time we are too insignificant to be the stewards of the Earth; it is only in the brief span of human time that we can think of ourselves in this way. Nature is vaster, more complex and more powerful than we will ever be able to understand. We acknowledge this when we use 'nature' to mean all of life's forms in interaction with the Earth's inorganic processes. Immense diversity exists within an essential unity. This concept of nature tends to lead the mind in one of two directions: the scientific or the religious.

The religious direction is essentially mystical. Nature is either a manifestation of God in some way, or, in the pantheistic version, it is imbued with the godhead in some way. In this view, nature's reality is not doubted, but there is either a greater reality behind it, or it is itself subsumed in a greater reality.

Science, by contrast, measures nature, considers its subsidiary parts, and constructs overarching theories about it. Organic chemistry has revealed how living cells replicate through the genes. This discovery in turn has provided a unitary base for understanding nature, since DNA is the self-replicating genetic material in the cells of *all* organisms in *all* five kingdoms of conventional scientific classification: Monera (single-celled organisms devoid of organelles, such as bacteria); Protista (single-celled organisms with complex cells); Fungi; Plantae; and Animalia. All organisms, no matter how remote they may seem from each other now, share this inheritance from the origin of life in the oceans 3.5 or more billion years ago. The neo-Darwinian synthesis of evolutionary theory and genetics has shown how this diversity came to exist by unravelling the mechanisms that underly speciation – the evolution and proliferation of species.

A twist to this scientific exploration of unity in diversity in nature has been the Gaia hypothesis of James Lovelock. Lovelock has done a service in reminding us of the interconnectedness of nature. In this view, nature is a self-regulating system governed by a series of negative feedback loops. In geological time we can probably do little to harm it, but in human time we may be causing the system to trip temporarily into a positive feedback loop which may have serious consequences for us as a species and for many other species with whom we temporarily share the Earth.

But Lovelock goes further and suggests that the Earth – in its inorganic as well as its organic aspects – may itself be a single superorganism that regulates itself. Here science swings out into the world of religion, feeding those New Age travellers and fellow-travellers who are hungry for mysticism. If the Earth is 'Gaia' – 'Mother' – then we are both part of 'her' and also her 'children'. It is honey in the rock for the sentimental end of the environmental movement which prefers infantilism to thought. This was not Lovelock's intention but it has been an unfortunate result of the extended version of his hypothesis.

Mostly we think of nature as it is *now* – something familiar, scarcely changing at all. This view comes loaded with the inheritance of more than ten thousand years of human experience, during which time society was overwhelmingly rural, and life was governed by work on the land. The seasons changed but returned in an ever-recurring cycle, nature forever different in its aspects but in its deep structure forever the same.

However, the four seasons and their attendant iconography have a diminished hold on our imaginations now compared with even forty years ago. Before the age of mass household refrigeration and the mass distribution of food through supermarkets, food in Europe tended to be local and seasonal. Basic foods such as potatoes were stored against the winter, but those that were more perishable, such as strawberries and other fruits, were available fresh only during their short local growing season. Today we can buy strawberries for most of the year, flown in from as far away as California and Chile; we pick off the shelf a punnet of out-of-season green beans from Kenya without a thought – for in machine-civilization we have done all that we can to obliterate the seasons and their influence on our lives. We cannot obliterate the light and dark, the warmth and cold of summer and winter, but that is about all. Seasonal sports such as tennis and swimming can be indulged in all year round with indoor courts and pools. Holidays too: in the deepest mid-winter, technology transports us to sunshine and summer in a matter of hours. To the urban dweller, nature is more static than ever before.

of peelings, *reason*
not,

But, while we may feel this at a visceral level, if we stop to think about it and inform ourselves, we know that nature is in truth quite different. The sense of its being static or cyclic on a small scale is a function of the human time-scale on which we customarily operate. In turn, this intuitive sense of time and space is a product of our own evolutionary development – a function of our height, age-expectancy and metabolism as a species.

We can understand from experience the length of time that is a year, a decade, and even by extension a century. We can just about conceive – in the sense of experience imaginatively – the 10,000-year period that constitutes the history of civilization from the beginnings of agricultural settlement. But beyond that the mind begins to flag. The Neanderthals died out 30,000 years ago, a mere 20,000 years before the development of agriculture by *Homo sapiens*. Yet we cannot conceive of that length of time other than as an abstraction. *Homo erectus*, our nearest ancestor species, existed for *c.* 1,400,000 years against our species' 100,000 years so far. The mind fails – it is like peering into a great distance and listening intently, to silence. The relics for the whole of this period of *Homo erectus*'s stone-tool culture barely changed at all, scattered through the strata of 1.4 million years.

But that is only the beginning of geological time which is measured in millions of years and is conventionally divided by geologists into four great epochs whose boundaries are determined by mass extinctions of the organisms then living. These are the Cenozoic (the present to 65 million years ago (myr)); the Mesozoic (65 to 245 myr); the Palaeozoic (245 to 570 myr); and the Precambrian (570 to the origin of the Earth *c.* 4.5 billion years ago).[1]

It is on this scale – which we can conceive intellectually, but which we can barely comprehend in terms relevant to ourselves – that nature must be measured. Nature on the human time-scale is like a single frame in a feature film. What seems so permanent to us is in fact provisional and constantly changing. Plate tectonics push continents together and tear them apart; mountain ranges like the Himalayas are thrown up by the

---

[1] See the geological chart accompanying the essay 'Limits to imagination'.

collision of plates; subduction zones destroy continental shelves; mountains are reduced by erosion to the level of plains; huge shallow seas like the one that extended from modern Alaska through the American Mid-West to Mexico in the Cretaceous period (65–146 myr) dry up.

And such convulsive events, immeasurably slow on the human time-scale, but not on the scale of geological deep time, helped shape and change nature so profoundly that if we could go back in time we would hardly recognize it. The great Carboniferous forests that flourished 280–345 myr ago consisted entirely of species of ferns. Other plants included club mosses and horse tails (and mosses in the upper half of the period), but no flowering plants and so no trees in our sense. Insects begin to appear in the Carboniferous, but at nowhere near the abundance that begins with the Jurassic (195 myr). There were spiders and scorpions, centipedes and millipedes. Amphibians were more numerous as species than they are now, and the end of the period saw the first reptiles, but there were no birds and no mammals. Except for the buzz of insects, the forests of the Carboniferous must have been eerily silent.

Transported back to such a time, we could probably survive, but how would we feel? We are part of nature now, the product of its present, impermanent, constantly changing aspect. We will surely become extinct, for that is the fate of all species, and almost certainly we are in the throes of a mass extinction now, the seventh since the Cambrian, and this one human-induced. If this four-dimensional view of nature through deep time could only become current in our general culture – that is, become truly internalized rather than manipulated and marketed as dinosaur-mania – then perhaps we could wake up from our present sleep-walk.

The revelation of nature in deep time is one of the great achievements of the human mind. Yet in a way it still leaves us with a question as to what nature is. Without order we cannot easily perceive meaning, and in order to understand nature science has been obliged to systematize it. A fundamental tool in this process is the system of nomenclature devised by Linnaeus, which sorts living organisms into hierarchies of relationships: in ascending order, species, genus, family, order, class, phylum, and kingdom. The Linnaean system is effective because it corresponds to genuine relationships in nature. But as a system it is a human construct and when we use it, or when we discuss nature in terms of evolutionary theory, we are mediating nature through an idea of it, an abstraction, no matter how frequent the reference points in nature itself.

Change the system and you change what you see. Nature in the fourteenth century was essentially Aristotelian. Species were static, brought into being at a single instant by God's act of creation, and existing until the end of the world. Someone looking at nature in 1395 would have seen the same birds and animals, fishes and plants and trees as we do now. That person's sense impression of them would have been similar to our own. (Proof of this is in the marvellously accurate depiction of birds to be found in some illuminated manuscripts.) But nature would not have *seemed* the same intellectually, because the Aristotelian view, adjusted by Christian theology, imposed a system that distorted nature in a particular direction, cramming it into what are to us crude categories and an impossibly truncated time-scale.

Evolutionary theory has stood up to intense examination for over one hundred and thirty years. There is such a thing as progress towards truth, but scientific truth is necessarily provisional. The view we have of nature now is wonderfully capacious and at the same time precise. It seems to correspond ever more exactly to what nature is. Yet so would the Aristotelian system have seemed to that hypothetical person in 1395. Although we have reason to be confident, we cannot be entirely sure that we have got it right. Nature in 600 years' time, if there are humans to observe it, may seem radically different from how it appears to us now.

2

Limits to imagination

In February 1992, the Royal Society and the US National Academy of Sciences issued a communiqué on Population Growth, Resource Consumption and a Sustainable World in which they expressed the opinion that 'if current predictions of population growth prove accurate and patterns of human activity on the planet remain unchanged, science and technology may not be able to prevent either irreversible degradation of the environment or continued poverty for much of the world'.

Such a statement may seem surprising, coming as it does from two of the world's most prestigious scientific academies which by nature tend to be conservative, but it reflects the growing pessimism of scientists working in various disciplines concerned with the environmental and population crises – a pessimism equally evident in the darkening tone of articles in journals such as *Scientific American* and *Nature*.

When they address the question of what science can do to reverse current trends, the Royal Society and the National Academy make an observation which is perhaps the most significant in the communiqué: 'Greater attention . . .', they say,

> needs to be given to understanding the nature and dimension of the world's biodiversity. Although we depend on biodiversity for sustainable productivity, we cannot even estimate the number of species of organisms – plants, animals, fungi, and microorganisms – to an order of magnitude. We do know, however, that the current rate of reduction in biodiversity is unparalleled over the past 65 million years.

And they conclude: 'The loss of biodiversity is one of the fastest moving aspects of global change, is irreversible, and has serious consequences for the human prospect in the future.'

By 'to an order of magnitude', they mean that we really have no idea how many species inhabit the Earth, with estimates varying between 30 and 80 million. What we do know is that species are becoming extinct at an ever increasing rate and that in the tropics, certainly, many species are dying out before they have even been identified by humans.

The real significance of the statement, though, is in the choice of 65 million years as the basis of comparison for anything similar in the past. For 65 million years ago saw the last, in the sense of latest, mass extinction in the history of life on Earth, at the Cretaceous-Tertiary boundary (usually abbreviated to K-T). In other words, the Royal Society and the National Academy are suggesting that the current rate of species extinction is such that we may ourselves be in the grip of a mass extinction.

The K-T is lodged in our minds because that particular event is associated with the demise of the dinosaurs, but also because recently it has been the subject of a fascinating scientific debate which has been widely reported by the media. This arose from the hypothesis of Walter and Luis Alvarez, first propounded in 1980, that 65 million years ago the Earth was hit by an extra-terrestrial object which triggered the K-T extinction. They were drawn to this conclusion by the discovery of an iridium anomaly or 'spike' right at the Cretaceous-Tertiary boundary. Iridium is rare in the Earth's crustal rocks (though it is found in association with vulcanism) but common in extra-terrestrial objects such as meteorites.

The concentration of iridium was first discovered at a site in Italy, then at other K-T boundary sites in Denmark, New Zealand and other locations around the world. Global distribution of iridium at the K-T suggested only one explanation to the Alvarezes – an extra-terrestrial object (bolide) *c.* 10 km in diameter which would have impacted at a speed of 55,000 m.p.h., causing an explosion more devastating than the detonation of all the world's nuclear arsenals. The consequences would have included the flash-fire of entire forests, a global pall of smoke and dust blocking out the sun and shutting down photosynthesis, a sharp drop in temperature, acidified snow and rain polluting lakes, rivers and even the oceans where the acid would have killed the calcareous plankton at the base of the ocean food chain. Extinction according to this scenario would have been massive and, in geological terms, swift.

The impact theory has been extensively debated. The vulcanism that produced the massive Deccan Traps in India over a million-year period at the end of the Cretaceous has been adduced as a possible source of the iridium. But while this may account for some of it, the discovery of shocked grains of quartz (associated with the effects of a massive explosive force) with the iridium at several K-T sites has convinced most geologists and paleontologists that the impact theory is, in broad outline, correct.

The Alvarezes went on to expand their theory in an attempt to account for all the major mass extinctions of the geological past by suggesting that the Earth is struck by extra-terrestrial bolides in a 26-million-year cycle. This was also widely reported by the media, including the hypothetical mechanism(s) for such a periodicity, such as an as yet undiscovered companion star to the sun, dubbed Nemesis, whose orbit approaches the sun every 26 million years, sending showers of comets on a collision course with Earth.

Reporting on science by the media is patchy at best, but it is relevant to ask why the impact theory at the K-T and its hypothetical extension as an explanation of *all* mass extinctions, has attracted so much popular attention, while countervailing arguments (which I shall come to later) have been decidedly under-reported, if not ignored. One reason is obvious. A massive impact by an object from outer space makes good copy. So does the idea, with its science-fiction overtones, of a 'death star' on its 26-million-year orbit round the sun.

But apart from sensationalism, the impact theory has a deeper appeal in that it locks into Western culture's tendency to think in millenarian terms. While it may be coincidental that the Alvarezes published their hypothesis in the last-but-one decade of our millennium, it is no accident that it appealed to the public imagination. An 'impact winter' of the kind proposed by the hypothesis is remarkably similar to the 'nuclear winter' which scientists were computer-modelling in the early 1980s and which Jonathan Schell did so much to popularize in his bestseller *The Fate of the Earth* (1982).

Geological Chart

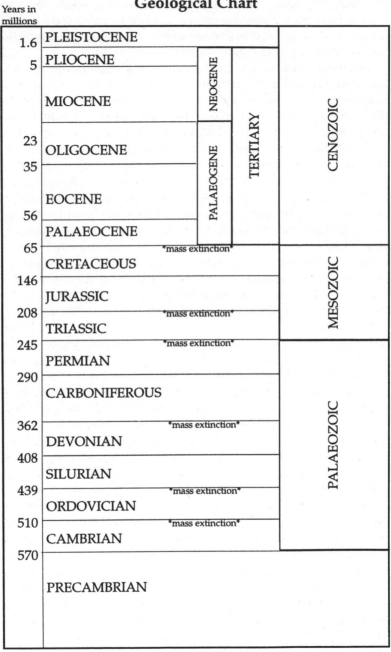

Years in millions

1.6	PLEISTOCENE				
5	PLIOCENE	NEOGENE	TERTIARY	CENOZOIC	
	MIOCENE				
23	OLIGOCENE	PALAEOGENE			
35					
	EOCENE				
56	PALAEOCENE				
65	*mass extinction*				
	CRETACEOUS			MESOZOIC	
146	JURASSIC				
208	*mass extinction*				
	TRIASSIC				
245	*mass extinction*				
	PERMIAN			PALAEOZOIC	
290	CARBONIFEROUS				
362	*mass extinction*				
	DEVONIAN				
408	SILURIAN				
439	*mass extinction*				
	ORDOVICIAN				
510	*mass extinction*				
	CAMBRIAN				
570	PRECAMBRIAN				

Millenarianism is so deeply a part of our cultural make-up that, as we approach AD 2000, it would be surprising if there were not a surge of apocalyptic prophesies and fears. Moreover, since in the West we live in an overwhelmingly secular society, it is also no surprise that this takes a material rather than a transcendental form.

In 1992 many looked to the Second Coming and the beginning of Christ's 1000-year reign on Earth as prophesied in the Revelations of St John the Divine. In 1992, global warming, acid rain, ozone layer depletion, desertification, rainforest loss, pollution of lakes, rivers and seas are thrown at us again and again by the media in what amounts to an apocalyptic vision, until in the end the mind can take no more and in self-defence makes itself numb. *Angst* and mass panic, hedonism and false gods are part of the *Zeitgeist* as they always are in a millenarian phase.

But periodicity in the impact hypothesis has perhaps yet another hidden appeal. For though some American astronomers have begun to monitor extra-terrestrial objects whose orbits might bring them on a collision course with Earth, while others, Dr Strangelove-like, talk of arming space rockets with nuclear warheads to blast threatening asteroids off course, there is an air of unreality about this – it is, as most people must see, science fiction, not science.

Yet the extra-terrestrial bodies *are* there and more and more of them are being identified by astronomers, and some are on orbits that will eventually bring them into a collision course with Earth. (Readers will remember reports of the small asteroid, only 5–10 metres in diameter which passed as close as 100,000 miles to the Earth in January 1991. Such an object would have equalled *c*. 40 kilotons of TNT.[1])

It may seem perverse, but such events and such knowledge almost come as a relief (I believe) to the late-modern mind, embattled as it is in an ecological mire of its own making. For the bad news carried daily by the media has an underlying message – that *we* are to blame. Guilt is one of the few lasting legacies of

---

[1] I.e. about three times the energy of the atomic bomb dropped on Hiroshima. (Duncan Steel, 'Our asteroid-pelted planet', *Nature*, 28 November, 1991.)

the Judaeo-Christian tradition in our secular culture. It is something which activist movements like Greenpeace are adept at manipulating. But I am not sure they are wise in doing so. For no matter how hard the individual tries – using Ecover products, unleaded petrol, 'adopting' a whale – the news still gets worse, compounding our collective sense of guilt and helplessness until it begins to thicken into despair. (The naming of the putative twin star to the sun 'Nemesis' after the Greek goddess of retribution seems to me deeply symptomatic.)

Many turn to hedonism, of course, as a means of escape from thought, something which, in any case, is not only encouraged but is essential to the capitalist market economy. None the less, it can seem a relief to be told that the last great mass extinction 65 million years ago was caused by an extra-terrestrial bolide impact, that inner space is littered with orbiting debris that must one day produce a similar event, and that there is nothing we can do about it. For if that is how mass extinctions occur, we are absolved of responsibility on the one hand, while on the other, if we think of a 'Nemesis' star orbiting mercilessly through space to end in our destruction, we can, in a way, feel absolved of our guilt. For that which we have done, we will be punished.

The impact theory, however, has not swept all before it to provide a comprehensive mechanism for mass extinction in the geological past. The extended hypothesis in particular is in trouble. It is difficult to reconcile the putative 26-million-year periodicity, for instance, with the geological record. Iridium, the clearest evidence for a bolide impact, has only been found in association with some extinction events, and in a context which, it seems, may suggest terrestrial geo-chemical processes.[2] Moreover, despite an active search, no companion star has so far been discovered, nor have astronomers been able to confirm any other extra-terrestrial mechanism for *periodic* impacts. The hypothesis still has its supporters, among them the eminent palaeontologist David M. Raup, but in general it has fallen into disfavour.

[2] Debra C. Colodner, Edward A. Boyle, John M. Edmond and John Thompson, 'Post-depositional mobility of platinum, iridium and rhenium in marine sediments', *Nature* (30 July, 1992).

Even at the K-T where there *was* an impact explosion, the original model proposed by the Alvarezes has had to be refined. The effects seem to have been worse in the northern than the southern hemisphere, for instance, so that the 'impact winter' may have been less severe than originally predicted. It may have been patchy – devastating in some regions but less so in others.

But most importantly, the mass extinction at the end of the Cretaceous is beginning to seem a more complex event than the impact theory would allow. As Niles Eldredge observes in *The Miner's Canary*, the Alvarezes effectively operate within ecological time, that is, days, months, years or at most decades, not within geological time with its scale of thousands, hundreds of thousands and millions of years. The impact theory in its most extreme form implies in Eldredge's words 'an immediate and utterly catastrophic event'.

This, however, is contradicted by the geological record. It is becoming clear, for example, that numerous species over many genera were in trouble for hundreds of thousand of years and in some cases millions of years before the bolide impact. As Robert Bakker has shown in *The Dinosaur Heresies*, dinosaur genera were in decline for several million years in the Upper Cretaceous with consequent loss of species diversity. The same is true for the ammonites, 'the very hallmark of Mesozoic life in the seas' (Eldredge). They too show a steady overall decline in species diversity during the Upper Cretaceous, even though, as with the dinosaurs, some species flourished. Only one thing is certain – flourishing or not, the dinosaurs and ammonites all were wiped out suddenly at the K-T.

What seems to be emerging is a picture of a mass extinction in the Upper Cretaceous stepped over perhaps several hundred thousand years, with the bolide impact at the K-T providing the *coup de grâce* to a broad range of species across many genera, many of which were already in trouble.[3] The end result was, however, equally severe. David Raup has calculated the percentages of taxa living in the later Cretaceous but dying out at the K-T as follows: classes, 1 per cent, orders, 10 per cent, families, 14 per cent, genera, 38 per cent, species, 65–70 per cent.

[3] Niles Eldredge gives an excellent overview in *The Miner's Canary: Unravelling the Mysteries of Extinction* (Prentice Hall, 1991).

(Devastating as the K-T extinction was, it is worth remembering that during the greatest mass extinction yet, at the Permo-Triassic 245 million years ago, a massive 96 per cent of marine species are estimated by David Raup to have become extinct.)

Sudden events like the K-T bolide impact appeal to us because they operate, in terms of effects, over a relatively short time-span which we can all relate to. But if, as Niles Eldredge and others argue, mass extinctions in the geological record all took place over hundreds of thousands and even, in the case of the Permo-Triassic, over several *million* years, it is tempting to ask what the term *mass* extinction really means, and in what way we as a species could possibly be implicated in one (except as victims). For the Permo-Triassic event appears to have taken place over a period at least as long as the entire evolutionary history of our genus, Homo.

The answer, of course, is partly that a few hundred thousand years are as nothing in what John McPhee has called deep time – the time-span by which geological and evolutionary change is measured. What we would consider accurate dating in 'our' time is something else in deep time. At the K-T, for instance, measurements to within half a million years are considered 'good'.

In geological deep time the loss of 65–70 per cent of species within several hundred thousand years is catastrophic and 'sudden', contrasting starkly with what David Jablonski has called 'background extinction'. Species are constantly becoming extinct, either directly or through the pseudo-extinction of phyletic development – the slow evolution of one species into another known as chronospecies, as may have happened between our immediate ancestor *Homo erectus* and early *Homo sapiens*. All species eventually become extinct in one way or the other, and as Raup has pointed out, a species that lasts 10 million years has done exceptionally well. Most die out here and there, however, over the millions of years that separate mass extinctions, as part of the background. Mass extinctions cut across this, decimating organisms 'suddenly' and not merely at the level of species and genera but, as at the K-T, right up the taxonomic scale to orders and classes.

Such a collapse is of course catastrophic but it also opens up possibilities for those organisms that manage to survive. As everyone knows, the final extinction of the dinosaurs at the K-T made available a wide range of ecological niches for the mammals which diversified rapidly into numerous branching genera and species, one twig of which eventually led to us.

But if extra-terrestrial impacts have only played a key role (as many palaeontologists, though not all, now believe) in one mass extinction, what other mechanism or mechanisms could be adduced to explain the phenomenon?

Niles Eldredge, among others, believes that a general theory of extinction has to encompass climate change, especially global cooling, which restricts habitat and acts as a trigger for waves of extinction in the tropics where numerous species thrive in very narrow ecological niches. For such species, specialization is an advantage while conditions are favourable – but it leaves them vulnerable; they tend to become extinct more quickly as part of background extinction than do more versatile generalist species associated with temperate latitudes, and when conditions change adversely during periods of global cooling, loss of narrow niches makes them highly susceptible to extinction – there is simply nowhere to retreat to and no time for evolutionary adaptation to new conditions.

The causes of global cooling (and consequent habitat loss, especially in tropical and subtropical zones) are complex and probably differ from period to period, but they include plate tectonics during periods of increased sea-floor spreading, and glaciation, each of which has a drastic impact on sea-level which in turn affects climate (Eldredge).

Yet interesting as this may be, it is still relevant to ask what it all has to do with us and why the Royal Society and the National Academy of Sciences should hint at a human-induced collapse in biodiversity comparable, perhaps, to that at the K-T?

Ironically, only a few years ago we would probably have found palaeontologists agreeing. 'For years,' writes Niles Eldredge in his Prologue to *The Miner's Canary*, 'I paid no particular attention to extinction, generally preferring to emphasize the positive side of my data: what trilobites can tell me about the nature of the evolutionary process.' But, he adds,

> I am also a living, breathing citizen of this planet. I cannot help but sense the growing alarm that my colleagues at the American Museum of Natural History have over the state of the world's local ecosystems

– leading to the loss of species after species of their favorite creatures. And, as an ordinary citizen, I cannot help but react to the nonstop media bombardment, the almost constant stream of unbelievably bad news about the state of the very local environment in which I live with my family and friends.

The Miner's Canary was the result of this realization – a fascinating synthesis of current thinking on extinction in the geological past and an exploration of what light this can throw on the environmental crisis of our times.

To understand how we could be involved *actively* in a possible mass extinction instead of passively as one of its many victims, we need to know more about ourselves *as* a species, and that involves understanding our evolutionary history as a member of the family Hominidae and the only living species of the genus Homo. As with extinction theory, a branch of palaeontology has taken on an uncharacteristically urgent and contemporary significance.[4]

As is commonly known, three of the most important developments in hominid evolution have been bipedalism, opposable thumbs and increased brain size in relation to body size. The latter is particularly impressive, with endocranial capacity increasing on average, according to Richard G. Klein, from 415 cc for *Australopithecus afarensis* (our earliest known hominid ancestor), to 630 cc for *Homo habilis*, to 850–900 cc increasing to 1050–1100 cc for our immediate ancestor *Homo erectus*, to 1400 cc for humans living today.

Arising out of these three evolutionary developments is a fourth, the most critical of all – culture. The culture of the earliest species of the genus Homo can only be inferred from artefacts found in association with their fossilized bones, which in the case of *H. habilis* and *H. erectus* are effectively limited to stone implements. The earliest stone tools, found in East and Southern Africa, are currently dated at between 2,400,000 and 2,500,000

[4] This section is much indebted to Richard G. Klein's *The Human Career: Human Biological and Cultural Origins* (University of Chicago Press, 1989), and Jared Diamond's *The Rise and Fall of the Third Chimpanzee* (Verso, 1991).

years and are associated with *Homo habilis*. It is an open question as to whether the contemporary hominid *Australopithecus robustus* also used primitive tools (Klein).

What is striking about them is their conservative nature. *H. habilis* produced the same primitive tools over thousands and thousands of years and across a wide geographical area, and while different stone tool industries are identified with *H. erectus* and the Neanderthals, this is equally true for them. The Mousterian Industrial Complex, for instance, associated with Neanderthals but also with early anatomically modern humans, was extraordinarily conservative. There is not even any evidence for experiment with similar tools in other media such as wood or bone, and no evidence for anything that might be interpreted as art or decoration.

> The general implication is that Mousterian/MSA [Middle Stone Age] people were behaviourally more conservative than their successors, with a limited ability to innovate even in the face of significant environmental variability through time and space. At least tentatively, it seems reasonable to propose that the behavioural limitations implied by Mousterian/MSA artifacts were linked to biological distinctions versus fully modern people ... (Klein)

During this long period – over 2 million years – the various species of Homo lived as hunter-gatherers (mostly probably as gatherers and scavengers because of their primitive tool-making capacity). They would have been integrated in local ecosystems where, because of their small numbers, they would have played a relatively minor role.

However, all this changed with the evolution of anatomically modern humans between *c.* 200,000 and 50,000 years ago, for it is during this period and in association with *Homo sapiens* that hominid culture erupted in a spectacular way with spectacular results:

> Prior to the emergence of modern people, the human form and human behaviour evolved together slowly, hand in hand. Afterwards, fundamental evolutionary change in body form ceased, while behavioural (cultural) evolution accelerated dramatically. The implication is that the modern human form – or, more precisely, the

modern human brain – permitted the full development of culture in the modern sense and that culture then became the primary means by which people responded to natural selection pressures. (Klein)

The significance of this cannot be overestimated, for as Klein goes on to observe:

As an adaptive mechanism, culture is not only far more malleable than the body, but cultural innovations can accumulate far more rapidly than genetic ones; and the result is that in a remarkably short time the human species has transformed itself from a relatively rare, even insignificant large mammal to the dominant life form on the planet.

And this is where the question of our involvement in extinction – even mass extinction – begins. For the exponential growth of human culture also led to an increase in population size and a steady geographic expansion. Though *Homo erectus* had spread out of Africa into Europe and the Near and Far East, it was none the less in the form of small bands, crucially limited by the narrow confines of their near-static culture. Whether in Africa or Java, *H. erectus* would have been a *part* of the local ecosystem, not the master of it.

The geographical spread of anatomically modern humans, however, which began *c.* 100,000 years ago, heralded the beginnings of a different kind of relationship to the local environment. The cultural advances which they took with them included superior stone tools and implements as well as artefacts in bone and wood. They included a great advance in weaponry, with consequent refinements in hunting techniques, as a result of which, for the first time, a species of the genus Homo appears to have been implicated directly in the extinction of other species.

Modern hunter-gatherers have become an emblem for some environmentally minded people of sustainability – humans living in harmony with their surroundings. But while this is true for some groups, it now seems more and more likely that this notion is the last twist of the Rousseauan myth of the Noble Savage, and as such the product of our own culture rather than a reflection of historical reality. For as more evidence is collected by palaeontologists and archaeologists, it is becoming clear that every phase of anatomically modern human expansion has gone hand in hand with a wave of extinctions of other large animals.

Jared Diamond recently surveyed the evidence for this in the Pacific islands.[5] At the time the Polynesians reached Hawaii about fifty bird species suddenly went extinct, and the same pattern is to be found in every island that has so far been studied palae-ontologically. Evidence of this is also accruing from the Americas, where the extinction of a wide range of large mammals in the late Pleistocene (see chart) appears to be related in successive waves to the spread of humans south from what is now Alaska. While there is some debate as to the significance of this, there is a growing body of opinion which would support Diamond's assertion that the evidence 'suggests that wherever anatomically and behaviour-ally modern *Homo sapiens* has reached land previously unoccupied by humans – whether a continent or an island – an extinction spasm of naive large prey has resulted'.

Our role as agent of extinction on the grand scale, though, did not really begin until the development of agriculture about 10,000 years ago. This provided an enlarged food base which in turn led to an increase in population which has continued ever since, albeit unevenly, in response to technological development. For one of the biological constraints acting on our species appears to be that humans, like other species, respond to increased food production on the Darwinian principle that a population always lives at or near the maximum that its resource base allows, all things being equal (Eldredge).

This, together with other cultural developments in fields such as medicine, has led to the crisis in world population with which we are faced now. It has also led to current fears that we may be involved as active agents in a mass extinction event. For it is not so much that humans are hunting animals to extinction (though of course we are doing that as well) but that our insatiable need for more land is destroying *habitat* on such a scale and in such a short space of time that we are on the verge (some would say in the middle) of a period of extinction equivalent to that at or near the K-T. David Raup estimated species loss at 65–70 per cent for

[5] 'Twilight of Hawaiian birds', *Nature* (10 October 1991). See also his 'Twilight of the Pygmy Hippos', *Nature* (3 September 1992) for evidence of human-induced extinctions on the Mediterranean islands.

the Cretaceous-Tertiary event. In *The Rise and Fall of the Third Chimpanzee*, Jared Diamond, one of the world's leading zoologists, estimates that on current trends, 'probably over half of existing species will be extinct or endangered by the middle of the next century, when this year's crop of human babies reaches the age of sixty'. If this is true, it takes us into the league of mass extinctions of the geological past.

What is to be done? Niles Eldredge has observed that we are unusual as a genus in that our success as *generalists* is based on a number of rare specializations, noted earlier – bipedalism, opposable thumbs and enlarged brain size in ratio to body size (including, in *Homo sapiens*, an enlarged cerebrum as compared with Neanderthals).

This in turn, as we have seen, led to our culture-driven development, beginning *c.* 100,000 years ago, rather slowly, but growing exponentially in the last 250 years through astonishing advances in science and technology. The positive and negative effects of such growth are generally well known by now, but they have also affected our ways of perceiving reality which are less easy to come at. Most significant is the way in which we are driven by the all-consuming idea of progress.

Whereas up to roughly the middle of the eighteenth century European culture looked *back* to an imagined Golden Age (whether in Classical Greece and Rome, or in Eden), we have, since the industrial revolution, tended to look forward to the Golden Age to Come, and we still do so despite the collapse of the great revolutionary ideals of Marx. For Capitalism, too, in its modern industrial form, is a product of nineteenth-century idealism. Communism may be dead, but we still believe (or many of us would like to) in the greatest good of the greatest number through the operation of a market economy in conjunction with political democracy. As a result, since this ideal state has never been reached, there is a sense in which we do not live in the present, and have not done so for the past 200 years, but in an imagined future. As we develop, of course, that magical Golden Age to Come forever recedes, and as global crises rise to meet us, it is beginning to appear as delusive as the Golden Age that Was.

It would be nice to think that the exigencies of the present have at last forced us to abandon such delusions. Unfortunately, I do not think they have. We live in the age of technology, but also in the age of *planning*. We believe – or have done so until very recently – that we can plan our way out of almost anything. And perhaps this is our most dangerous self-delusion. Perhaps we have come up against one of the most fundamental limits to the nature of our species. Increased endocranial capacity and a developed cerebrum have led us to where we are, but it could be that our brains are not large enough to cope with the complex of crises which our own development has caused. It may be that although we as a species can perceive what is happening, the evolutionary limits on our endocranial capacity, and its special-ized functions, mean that we cannot change our behaviour sufficiently and quickly enough to avert ecological collapse.

In *The Blind Watchmaker*, Richard Dawkins makes the point that our minds have evolved in such a way that constraints are imposed on what we can perceive through our senses, which in turn, for everyday purposes, impose a limit on what we consider 'reality'. The human eye, for instance, can only detect a very narrow band of electromagnetic frequencies which we call 'light'. The same is true, he continues, of our perception of distance and time. Although physicists regularly calculate in picoseconds, geologists in millions of years, and astronomers in light years, we cannot really imagine such a time-scale. And, he goes on:

> Just as our eyes can see only that narrow band of electromagnetic frequencies that natural selection equipped our ancestors to see, so our brains are built to cope with narrow bands of sizes and times. Presumably, there was no need for our ancestors to cope with sizes and times outside the narrow range of everyday practicality, so our brains never evolved the capacity to imagine them. It is probably significant that our body size of a few feet is roughly in the middle range of sizes we can imagine. And our lifetime of a few decades is roughly in the middle range of times we can imagine.

And here, possibly, we reach an in-built evolutionary constraint on our ability to solve our current environmental crisis – we simply cannot *imagine* on the necessary time-scale. We pride ourselves on our ability to plan, but our plans are all framed by the limited time-scale suggested by Richard Dawkins, as are the political, social and economic structures we have developed to implement them. Democracies, typically, plan in terms of four to five years, as did the Russian Communists with their famous five-year plans. Even to think in terms of ten to fifteen years is considered 'long-term' planning in the world we inhabit.

But the situation in which we find ourselves now demands far more than that – it demands the imagination to plan in the context of 50 years, 100 years, even 500 years. And as soon as the words are on the page we can see how impossible this is. Our institutions are not designed to plan on such a time-scale, because we ourselves have not evolved to be able to imagine it.

No one can say for certain what the future will bring. The exponential growth of human culture may surprise us yet. But it may be, as I am tentatively suggesting here, that culture, which had seemed to free us from the constraints of *evolutionary* development, has come up against an unexpected, evolved trait of our genus – one which sets limits on the ways in which we can plan, and so influence, the future. It would be an irony if failure of imagination brought our extraordinary species to an end at last.

Postscript

Among other works consulted: Niles Eldredge, *Fossils: The Evolution and Extinction of Species* (Aurum, 1991) (this has magnificent photographs of fossils by Murray Alcossar); David M. Raup, *Extinction: Bad Genes or Bad Luck?* (W. W. Norton, 1991); Christopher McGowan, *Dinosaurs, Spitfires and Sea Dragons* (Harvard UP, 1983, rev. edn 1991); Colin Tudge, *Last Animals at the Zoo: How Mass Extinction Can Be Stopped* (Hutchinson Radius, 1991); Robert Bakker, *The Dinosaur Heresies* (1986; Penguin, 1988); John Terborgh, 'Why American songbirds are vanishing', *Scientific American* (May 1992); Richard Dawkins, *The Blind Watchmaker* (1986; Penguin 1988).

3

Against the warehouse keepers

To know a great poem only in translation is frustrating because you can never be sure how much of the original is there and how far its meaning has suffered a cultural shift in the uprooting from one language to another. For this reason alone the process of translation is provisional and endless, each generation of foreign readers needing to come at the original again and again in new translations that provide an interpretation for their time.

When the original is in a lesser-used language, translations are likely to be few and far between so that each new attempt is doubly welcome. When I wrote about the Swedish poet Harry Martinson's great space epic *Aniara* in *The King of Ashes* (1989) the only translation, by Hugh MacDiarmid and Elspeth Harley Schubert, had been out of print for fifteen years. I had read it in my final year as an undergraduate and the translated poem made a great impression on me. Since then I have come to read it several times in Swedish and the MacDiarmid/Schubert translation has seemed less and less satisfactory.

Outside Scandinavia, however, Harry Martinson is hardly known and the likelihood of a new translation to interpret the poem for the 1990s seemed remote. But in 1991 the small Swedish publisher Vekerum Förlag took the initiative and published a fresh version by the American translators Stephen Klass and Leif Sjöberg so that once again *Aniara* is available to English readers.

~

Aniara is a giant spaceship ferrying refugees to Mars from an Earth badly polluted by nuclear wars. It is forced off course in a near collision with an asteroid and plunges into deep space with its cargo of humanity on a voyage of no return. The poem, in 103 cantos, follows Aniara's inhabitants over the years as they experience what can only be called entropy of the spirit, until the last survivors meet their end, huddled round the 'mima' – part-computer, part-conscience and suffering intelligence, which had been their consolation, relaying images of life on Earth and elsewhere in the universe, until it receives pictures of a nuclear holocaust which brings humankind on our planet at last to an end – at which the mima itself breaks down irreparably. 'Och genom alla,' the poem ends, 'drog Nirvanas våg' (And through us all [in the new translation] Nirvana's currents ranged). Aniara hurtles on alone against an unchanging backcloth of the immensity of space with its galaxies and stars, the 'sarkofag', sarcophagus, of this remnant of the human species.

Though not strictly working-class, Harry Martinson (b. 1904) was brought up in straitened circumstances. His father, an unpredictable and violent man, and a heavy drinker, died of tuberculosis when Martinson was six. The same year his mother, finding herself pregnant by another man and her attempt at setting up a small business in ruins, fled to America with her eldest daughter, abandoning Harry and his other sisters. Martinson never saw her again.

He and his sisters became the responsibility of the parish. They were separated and allocated on a yearly basis to various farms, ostensibly to be fostered, though in reality as unacknowledged, unpaid help. On some farms Harry was treated kindly, on others with a roughness approaching brutality. He never forgot either. This period of his life is the subject of the semi-autobiographical novels *Nässlorna blomma* (The Nettles Are in Flower, 1935) and *Vägen ut* (The Way Out, 1936).

One consolation during this period was the village school, especially when, in the second form, he came in contact with the eccentric, talented Karl Johan Staaf who recognized Martinson's intelligence and fostered it. Contrary to most children's experience, school became a kind of home away from the farms for Martinson, a refuge of the mind. Another consolation was the old people's home where he was placed after running away from the farm of his last foster parents, and where the superintendent, Anna Almkvist, gave him some of the maternal love for which he longed.

But by his early teens he had already set his mind on running away to sea, with the underlying notion of somehow seeking out his mother in America. Martinson spent the first half of the 1920s as a cabin boy, stoker and deck hand, travelling the major sea-lanes of the world, jumping ship frequently to tramp hundreds of miles, as he did in South America, before signing on again with another ship, another company. This period of his life was an endless, aimless journey, as is suggested by the titles of the two travel books based on it – *Resor utan mål* (Journeys without a Goal, 1932) and *Kap Farväl!* (Cape Farewell!, 1933).

But by the end of the 1920s, he had given up the sea and returned to Sweden, unemployed, often on the road, living for a time in a home-made tent, begging sometimes, accepting hand-outs, going from office to office of the then numerous left-wing and union papers and journals with a sheaf of poems which he tried to sell to editors on the spot, making in this way a few kronor here, a few kronor there.

Determined on a literary career, Martinson was lucky enough to achieve recognition quickly. He was included in a much talked-about anthology, *Fem unga* (Five Young [Poets], 1929), and his first collection, *Spökskepp* (Ghost Ship, 1929) was well received, as was his second, *Nomad* (1931), and *Resor utan mål* a year later.

From then on Martinson was and remained a professional writer. Following a Scandinavian tradition, he was immensely productive across a range of genres – apart from the travel books and autobiographical novels, there were ten collections of lyric poetry, a novel set in the world of Swedish tramps, *Vägen till Klockrike* (The Way to Klockrike, 1948), four collections of *natur prosa* (for which 'nature prose' is an inadequate translation), two dramas, a semi-fictional account of his involvement in the Finno-Russian War, *Verklighet till döds* (Reality unto Death, 1940), and numerous articles of social and cultural criticism. At his death in 1978 he left a mass of material in manuscript, much of which has yet to be published.

~

This quick sketch of Harry Martinson's early life and literary output may seem to place him among the remarkable group of proletarian writers who rose to prominence in Sweden in the 1920s and 1930s. Martinson certainly shares with writers like Ivar Lo-Johansson a background of rural poverty, unskilled labour and autodidactism. But he never shared the left-wing ideology that marked off the proletarian writers as a group and which gave some, like his first wife, the novelist Moa Martinson, strong sympathies with Stalinist Russia.

Martinson saw too clearly what was not at all clear to many left-wing intellectuals at the time – that Marxist ideology as practised in Russia was little different from Nazism and Capitalism in its ruthless dehumanizing of people into the masses in the name of an idea. His earliest perception of this was in the stokeholds of the Western world's ships just after the First World War, which he describes unforgettably in *Resor utan mål* and *Kap Farväl!*. There, as he paced back and forth, shovelling coal in the furnaces, he experienced the dehumanizing nature of work in what he later came to call 'maskincivilisation' – machine-civilization. So many tons shovelled every day, travelling across the great seas of the Earth, yet limited like a peasant behind his plough to the endless pacing between coal bunker and furnace across the metal plates of the deck.

Work, in industrial society, he realized, was a limiting, not a liberating experience, and it made no difference if the superstructure was Capitalist, or one of the two great ideological wings of revolution in Europe, Nazism and Communism, for each was committed to massive programmes of industrialization – to machine-civilization – and both were ruthless in their suppression and regimentation of humanity. This may seem obvious now as regards Communist Russia, but it was not at all obvious to Communist sympathizers in the West, including Moa Martinson, in the early 1930s.

In 1934 Moa and Harry Martinson attended the All-Russia Congress of Writers in Moscow as members of the Swedish delegation of foreign writers and guests of the Soviet Government. The Congress made a great impression on them both, though in radically different ways. Moa returned to Sweden and immediately wrote a glowing newspaper article on her Russian experience. Harry waited six years before he published his version as a prologue to *Verklighet till döds* in 1940. Moa Martinson, who had never been out of Sweden before, was overwhelmed by the excitement of the journey, the lavish fêting of the 600 foreign guests. 'Roses, carnations, roses, carnations,' she wrote, 'in a rain over the guests.' She was roundly attacked in the press by both the Right and the Left.[1] The theme of the Congress was set by a quotation from Lenin: 'The writer is the engineer of the human soul.' This struck Martinson, the ex-seaman and tramp, more forcefully than the bouquets, ballet and theatre visits, the showcase factories and collective farms. In *Verklighet till döds*, he describes how author after author rose to speak as an engineer of the soul, always with a ritual obeisance to Stalin, whose absence designedly created an oppressive presence. Fear, in Martinson's eyes, was the dominant mood of the All-Russia Congress of Writers.

At one stage, the whole Congress was taken to witness a giant air show at an airfield on the steppe outside Moscow. By Harry Martinson's reckoning there were a million spectators. Huge portraits of Stalin were towed behind aeroplanes, hung from dirigibles. Bombers flew over the field with the same 'jätteporträtt av guden' (giant portrait of the god). Stunt planes looped the loop, squadron after squadron of fighters and bombers filled the sky. As a climax, countless parachutists descended on the airfield which left the American journalists present gasping. Capitalism met Communism. Cries of delight rose from the Hearst-Press journalists, 'Här kunde man kanske rentav göra sig en karriär som reporter.' (You could make a whole career for yourself as a reporter here.) But, had they not been blinded by the Capitalist version of the same 'maskin-civilisation', they would have realized that they were also witnessing something else:

Här fick de nu se hur det regnade ned moderna och av ultratekniken nyfrälsta ryska bönder från himmelen. Det regnade länge och det regnade många.

[1] Details from Sonja Erfurth, *Harry Martinsons 30-tal* (Bonniers, 1989). Details of his childhood are taken from Sonja Erfurth, *Harry Martinsons barndoms-värld* (1980; repr. Vekerum Förlag, 1989).

Here they saw how modern Russian peasants rained down from the heavens, newly saved by advanced technology. It rained long and it rained many.

Martinson never forgot this glimpse into the heart and mind of Stalinist Russia, and when Russia invaded Finland in 1939–40 he joined the Swedish Volunteer Corps fighting on the Finnish side. Although he was a pacifist by nature and in principle, he saw Finland's fight as the fight of Sweden and other small peoples against 'maskincivilisation'. Because of his poor health (he suffered periodically from tuberculosis) and his age, he was considered unfit to fight in the harsh conditions of the Winter War, but he acted as a courier at the front.

There on 12 March he experienced one small but emblematic example of machine-civilization's cynicism and barbarism. A cease-fire had been agreed by both sides for 11 a.m. However, the HQ of the 122nd Russian division decided to hold a 'little war finale'. 'Krigen skulla dansas ut' (The war was to be danced out). From dawn till 11 a.m., squadron after squadron of dive-bombers bombed Kemijärvi and Rovaniemi:

> Hus föllo samman, eldsvådor anställdes och mänskor dödades med byråkratisk punktlighet till fem i elva. Vid fronten höll de inte like noga. Deras bombningsuppvisning gick där over med nära tolv minuter.

> Houses collapsed, conflagrations were started, people were killed with bureaucratic punctuality until five-to-eleven. At the front, they weren't quite such good time-keepers. Their bombing display went overtime by about twelve minutes.

This was, as he realized, merely a continuation of the massive air show he had seen six years previously. 'Mod och skicklighet fattades inte i fartens tid och luftherraväldets tid – bara mänsklighet fattades.' (There was no lack of courage and skill in the age of speed, the age of domination of the skies – only humaneness was lacking.)

In his writing, Martinson held humanity in balance with nature. When he wrote *Resor utan mål*, he toyed with the idea of the 'world nomad', of a future in which humanity would be liberated from place and free to *be* anywhere. Partly this was an attempt to give some coherence to his own aimless years as a seaman. But though the image of the journey is there as a complex symbol in his work to the end, he came to see how profoundly his own sensibility had been shaped by the rural Sweden of his childhood.

Brought up on farms, Harry Martinson had no illusions about farm life. He knew how the back-breaking work on the land could brutalize people and make them in turn cruel to their kind. The heroes and heroines of his fiction are always the vulnerable – the orphaned Martin of the autobiographical novels, the brow-beaten women and girls of the remote farms, social outcasts such as the professional tramps of his childhood who people *Vägen till Klockrike*.

As a child, Martinson had felt kinship with such people; they were his kind. But he also found consolation away from humanity, on the heaths, in the conifer and birch woods, along the shores of the lakes and in the meadows. There, alone, he absorbed himself in the different world of nature which is the theme of so much of the lyric poetry and the 'natur prosa'. He retained to the end what most of us lose – the child's intense involvement with the minutiae of life among the grass-stalks which adults must bend to see, but which is vividly present to the eyes and ears of the child crawling in the insects' world, familiarly and secretly his own and boundlessly different. *Utsikt från en grästuva* (View from a Tussock, 1963) and *Tuvor* (Tussocks, 1973) are the titles of his last book of essays and penultimate collection of poems.

Harry Martinson was a Romantic, but he was not romantic about nature. Widely read in biology, he well understood the mechanics and the philosophical implications of a Darwinian view of the world. Some of his most memorable descriptions are of the dangerous microcosm of the insects, the ruthless hunting and killing taking place at our feet among the grass and flowers as we walk through a seemingly innocuous summer day's meadow.

But he could describe, too, the endless soughing of the wind in the great Swedish forests, the stillness that descends on a lake at dusk. Nature in its totality, amoral and beautiful, was the source of what must be called his religious feelings about life, though the term must be kept deliberately vague. He is closest perhaps to Robinson Jeffers, but without the latter's fierce delight in what he conceived of as a grandly inhuman god. Nature for Martinson was essential to what he called the human soul.

Martinson's reading in the sciences extended beyond biology to include astronomy and physics. This led to another of the formative experiences of his life. In January 1941, a Swedish Week was organized in German-occupied Copenhagen by the Danish Union of Writers. Martinson attended with his second wife Ingrid and managed to arrange a meeting with Niels Bohr at the Institute for Theoretical Physics. Bohr showed him the splitting of the atom in a Wilson cloud chamber. It made a deep impression on Martinson, who asked whether it would not be possible to make a powerful bomb out of this release of energy. Bohr replied that it would be so expensive that the cost of building such a bomb would be prohibitive. Martinson never forgot that answer. 'Ett par år senare,' he recalled years later, 'var han i fullt arbete på atombomben' (A couple of years later he was hard at work on the atom bomb).[2]

The swift development and use of the atom bomb by the Americans depressed Martinson greatly. Niels Bohr had been wrong. In mass society, cost is no object when something is willed by the people's leaders. Hiroshima and Nagasaki were landmarks of human inventiveness and inhumanity which have shadowed the world since. The destruction of those cities is part of the climate of the world of *Aniara*.

But Harry Martinson saw nuclear war in a wider context of machine-civilization, a logical outcome of our century's unswerving commitment to technological advance and material values, with the consequent systematic dehumanization of the individual into a member of the mass. As early as 1937 he wrote in *Svärmare och harkrank* (Hawk-moth and Crane-fly), his second collection of 'natur prosa', that

> Vi producera men bli själva produkter. Detta är bland annat modernismens inre tragik, ett slags varumästargärning som i längden belaster inte bara språket som hotar att spränges, men också psyket. Själva naturen undergår aktualitetsförvandlingar.

[2] Interview with Elly Jannes, reprinted in *Kring Aniara* (Vekerum Förlag, 1989); also Erfurth, *Harry Martinsons 30-tal*.

We produce but we also become products. This is part of modernism's inner tragedy, a kind of warehouse-keeping which in the long term not only weighs down language, which threatens to burst apart, but also the psyche. Nature itself is transformed by current developments.

Harry Martinson would not have been surprised that Russian soldiers used to clear highly radioactive debris in the immediate aftermath of Chernobyl were referred to by their masters as 'bio-robots', or that those who helped build the 'sarcophagus' over the reactor were termed 'liquidators'. 'Det allra värsta,' he observed in his interview with Elly Jannes in 1957, 'är at maskinerna trivialiserar lidelsen.' (The worst thing of all is that machines trivialize our feelings.)

In the post-war period, Martinson's thinking darkened considerably. The relentless pace of technological change which led to the exponential growth of the mass media, the rapid spread of the car, the hundred-and-one machines that were pressed upon a more than willing public as necessary to their lives, were undermining, he saw, all that he believed in. And to stand apart, as he did, and question these processes was to become an outcast. *Aniara* was widely acclaimed, but thereafter his reputation began to decline as he made his position *vis-à-vis* modern society increasingly clear to an audience that did not want to hear.

In 1960 he published a collection of poems, *Vagnen* (The Car). It contains a sequence in which the car is seen as the Juggernaut of the people in a materialist society, to which they willingly and blindly sacrifice themselves. *Vagnen* was poorly received by younger critics who accused Martinson of being a reactionary.[3]

When questioned about this in an interview with Matts Rying,[4] Martinson denied the charge. In mass society, he pointed out, you are not allowed to express a different opinion because you tread on people's toes. When he did this in *Vagnen*, 'Där stod små bilförardvärgar upp och yttrade vredgade ord' (Then small car-driver-dwarfs stood up and uttered angry words). He added

[3] Georg Svensson, *Harry Martinson som jag såg honom* (Alba, 1980).
[4] Reprinted in *Kring Aniara*.

sarcastically, 'Och recensenterna blev förargade och illa till mods, de har väl också varsin bil att sitta och åka i.' (And the reviewers were angry and uncomfortable – no doubt each of them has a car to drive about in.)

The materialism of 'maskincivilisation' pervades everything, even nature, as Martinson saw as long ago as the late 1930s. By the 1960s, nature, which meant so much to him and from which he believed we derive a necessary sense of beauty, was so invaded by machines that he could no longer take pleasure in it.

In his last book of prose, *Utsikt från en grästuva* (View from a Tussock), he explained in an essay called 'Brev' (Letter) why he could no longer write about nature in the old way. It was because the Swedish countryside had become for him, to all intents and purposes, destroyed by machines. Their noise invades the woods and the lakes, takes the pleasure out of a walk in the lanes:

> Ännu för bara tjugo år sedan kunde man finna befrielse i att gå till fots på en landsväg. Nu är den känslan omöjlig at nå. Man måste ständigt se upp, ständigt vara på sin vakt mot överraskningar, livsfaror, farter och bullermängder.

> Even just twenty years ago you could find relief by walking along a country lane. Now that feeling is impossible. You have to look up constantly, constantly be on guard against the unexpected, against dangers, speed and noise.

For these reasons, he continues, he has altogether given up taking walks in the lanes – 'Det har närapå blivit en form av förnedring.' (It has almost become a form of degradation.)

In the 1960s and 1970s, when armchair Marxism was the fashion among young intellectuals, Martinson steadily lost popularity. He continued to write but refused to publish. After *Vagnen*, eleven years went by before the appearance of another collection of poems, *Dikter om ljus och mörker* (Poems about Light and Darkness, 1971). After this, only a small collection of lyrics, *Tuvor* (1973) for his publisher's book club, appeared in his lifetime.

In his latter years he became deeply embittered. Asked by Matts Rying (in the context of the reception of *Vagnen*) about his public, he replied that he had no public but that he wrote for one or two readers, or for the dead, such as Conrad, or Tolstoy, adding with a laugh, 'Men inte försöker jag främkalla hans astral krop. Jag bara berättar en sak for Tolstoj som är död' (But I'm not trying to call up his astral body. I just narrate something for Tolstoy who is dead).

Just before his own death in 1978, he was persuaded to prepare one last collection from the enormous number of unpublished poems he had written in the past decade. It appeared posthumously under the title *Längs ekots stigar* (Along the Echo's Paths).

I have tried to suggest something of the scope of Harry Martinson's work and the development of his life and ideas as a background to the new translation of *Aniara*. For although it is arguably his greatest poem, it has to be set beside the autobiographical novels and *Vägen till Klockrike* as well as the accumulative achievement of his lyric poetry. To read *Aniara* alone, I have come to learn, is like reading *The Waste Land* or *Heart of Darkness* without reference points to the work that went before and comes after.

So how good is the Klass/Sjöberg version? As I said, translation seems at once essential and impossible. There is only one *Aniara* and it is in Swedish. Language does not 'clothe' a poem's meaning, as the blurb to this translation half suggests. If that notion of poetry, derived from Classical rhetoric were true, then the essence of a poem could indeed be translated, given new clothes in another language, without too much loss. The trouble is that Keats's axiom 'That if Poetry comes not as naturally as the Leaves to a tree it had better not come at all' is right. The organic relation between a poem and the language that produced it defeats translation time and again.

Translation seems to me more like a map. If it is a good map, an experienced reader can re-create in his mind something of the landscape that must be there from the contours and symbols of the map's two-dimensional plane.

In these terms, Stephen Klass and Leif Sjöberg's translation is an excellent map of the great mindscape of *Aniara*. They take chances. Harry Martinson used a vide variety of verse forms in the poem from free verse to verse with intermittent rhyme, to tightly rhymed quatrains. Hugh MacDiarmid and Elspeth

Harley Schubert avoided rhyme altogether in their version, giving a false sense of the poem's forms. Against all the difficulties that rhyme entails, the Klass/Sjöberg translation is successful time and again in mapping, for the English-language reader, the formal intricacies of the original, and it is one of their greatest achievements. Occasionally there are lapses into a woodenness of phrase, but these are nothing when set against the enormity of the task.

Aniara has been called 'the star song of our time' in Sweden. Many of Harry Martinson's ideas, about nature, the destruction of the environment, even about the car, are seeing their time now, eighteen years after he died a bitter man. *Aniara* is not a poem without hope, but it is a poem with a warning. Many of the negative effects of the way we live, which he prophesied in the 1940s and 1950s, are now upon us. But *Aniara* is not merely a topical poem, it penetrates beneath the level of politics, technology and planning, with which many hope to fend off disaster, to examine the deep divisions within what he would call Western humankind's soul.

'Y bardd ydi'r unig ddyn rhydd mewn cymdeithas,' R. S. Thomas said recently. (The poet is the only free being in society.) Harry Martinson would have understood that, as he would have understood the endurance and bitterness such freedom implies. *Aniara* should be read, for it enacts what may be the last great journey of the human mind, and if not in Swedish, then in this excellent English translation which maps the spaceship as it journeys alone through space and time.

4

Fatalists of the new kind

The question 'What are we?' must at least be as old as the evolution 100,000 years ago of anatomically modern humans whose brain size and shape suggest that they would have had a capacity for consciousness similar to our own. For most of this (in human terms) long period of time our species sought answers in a proliferation of religious beliefs. In modern times, however, the question cannot be broached meaningfully without taking into account the domain of science and especially the neo-Darwinian synthesis of the biological sciences which has changed profoundly and most likely for ever the way in which we must regard ourselves.

Darwin himself was acutely aware of this 140 years ago when he agonized over the publication of his theory of evolution. So too were Christian opponents after the publication *The Origin of Species* in 1859, for both sides recognized that the stake was not merely the nature of nature but the nature of mankind.

Even today many draw back from the idea that human nature can be fully integrated into the Darwinian theory of the evolution of species by natural selection, for it is hard not to feel that this would somehow diminish us, involving as it must the abandonment of long-cherished notions of ourselves as beings who are part of nature certainly, but who are in a crucial way also different from other species, set for ever a little apart. Even those who otherwise consider themselves agnostic or non-religious hesitate to render up this last vestige of what might be called the sacred hypothesis of human nature. It is consequently not surprising that any discipline which attempts to demonstrate the reasons why we should do just that will come under attack from a number of directions and that any individual who promotes such ideas with vigour will be the object of opprobrium.

This is what has happened to sociobiology, one of the most exciting disciplines to have emerged from the neo-Darwinian synthesis of the past forty years, and to its most eminent proponent, the American biologist, Edward O. Wilson.[1] Many readers may be best familiar with Wilson as the author of *The Diversity of Life* (1993), a study of the present crisis in biodiversity and global ecology which was widely reviewed by the English press. His scientific reputation, however, rests on three books published in the 1970s, *The Insect Societies* (1971), *Sociobiology* (1975) and *On Human Nature* (1978). *The Insect Societies* is a detailed study of the biological origins and functions of complex behaviour in social insects – the ants and termites and social species of bees and wasps. *Sociobiology* arose as an obvious sequel: a wide-ranging survey of what was currently known about social species of animals from the insects to the mammals and – in a concluding chapter that was to become highly controversial – *Homo sapiens*. Developing out of that chapter, *On Human Nature* concluded what Edward Wilson has referred to as his trilogy, by placing human nature as a legitimate object of study firmly and unequivocally within the parameters of sociobiology.

Sociobiology – '. . . the systematic study of the biological basis of all social behaviour' (*Sociobiology*) – has been applied with great success by Wilson and others to the study of animals and by palaeoanthropologists seeking to understand behavioural patterns in early *Homo sapiens* and hominid predecessors such as *Homo erectus* and *Homo habilis*.

When it comes to modern human society, however, socio-

---

[1] See for example the concerted attack on Wilson and sociobiology by his fellow-biologist Stephen Jay Gould: 'Biological potential v. biological determinism', in *Ever Since Darwin* (1979; Penguin, 1980); *The Mismeasure of Man*, pp. 324ff. (1981; Penguin, 1984); 'Cardboard Darwinism', in *An Urchin in the Storm* (1988; Penguin, 1990). See also the parodic account of sociobiology (and neo-Darwinism generally) in Edward Goldsmith, *The Way* (Rider, 1992).

biology has conventionally given way to sociology, a very different discipline which, according to Wilson, is restricted to empirical description of phenotypic (i.e. individual) behaviour often in an intuitive way, 'without reference to evolutionary explanation in the true genetic sense' (*Sociobiology*). If it is ever to approach the deeper meaning of human behaviour, Wilson argues, sociology must integrate with biology, for the 'core of social theory' is the biological (that is, genetic) deep structure of our nature (*On Human Nature*).

And here of course is where sociobiology attracts head-on opposition, for it is one thing to apply the reductionist analysis of genetics to the study of animal behaviour and even the behaviour of early hominids. It is quite another when the same method of analysis is turned on ourselves. Scientific reduction is 'feared and resented', as Wilson notes: 'For if human behaviour can be reduced and determined to any considerable degree by the laws of biology, then mankind might appear to be less unique and to that extent dehumanized.' Perceiving this, perhaps, researchers in the social sciences and the humanities have been reluctant to engage with sociobiology, 'let alone surrender any of their territory'. But they are wrong, Wilson argues, on two counts: firstly because the 'method of reduction' in science is not the same thing as the 'philosophy of minimalism', and secondly because, like it or not, 'Biology is the key to human nature, and social scientists cannot afford to ignore its rapidly tightening principles' (*On Human Nature*).

The crucial question is to what *extent* is human behaviour genetically determined? Geneticists have had notable success, as in the isolation of the genetic basis of diseases such as Huntingdon's disease, but their claims often go much further to include genes for behavioural patterns ranging from criminality to alcoholism and to behavioural disorders such as schizophrenia and manic depression. Some go further still and claim a genetic orientation for aspects of behaviour generally thought to be clearly within the realm of culture, such as religiosity, political orientation and leisure interests. These claims are often hurriedly reported in the popular press. What is rarely reported is the fact that every such claim to date has been disproved or withdrawn. If there is a genetic component in such behavioural traits it does not reside in a single gene or group of genes but within such a complex array within the immensely complex human genome that they may never be identifiable. Moreover, even if they were identified, it might still never be possible to isolate their effect with the certainty necessary to influence them.[2] It is unlikely that we will ever isolate a 'gene for happiness' as some eugenicists have supposed.

The real case for genetic influence on human behaviour is more subtle. It is not so much that a one-to-one relationship exists between specific genes or sets of genes and specific behavioural patterns but that genes exert a complex indirect influence on behaviour. As Edward Wilson explains, we are not likely to find mutations 'of a particular sexual practice or mode of dress'. Instead, behavioural genes are likely to influence 'the ranges of the form and intensity of emotional responses, the thresholds of arousal, the readiness to learn certain stimuli as opposed to others, and the pattern of sensitivity to additional environmental factors that point cultural evolution in one direction as opposed to another.' Those who fear that the inroads of genetic determinism will undermine our concept of humanity and our self-esteem fail to understand the profound difference that exists between genetic determinism in humans and, for instance, in the social insects where 'development is confined to a single channel, running from a given set of genes to the corresponding single predestined pattern of behaviour'. When a sociobiologist looks at the genetic basis of behaviour in humans he sees a very different pattern which is 'circuitous and variable', in which 'human genes prescribe the *capacity* to develop a certain array of traits', a capacity which is itself highly variable: 'In some categories of behaviour, the array is limited and the outcome can be altered only by strenuous training – if ever. In others, the array is vast and the outcome easily influenced' (*On Human Nature*).

Even indirect genetic influence on human behaviour might, however, seem hard to prove, for has not biological evolution been superseded in humans by *culture* which develops at a rate far in excess of evolutionary-induced change? As a result, are not

[2] See John Horgan, 'Eugenics revisited: trends in behavioural genetics', *Scientific American* (June 1993); John Maddox, 'Wilful public misunderstanding of genetics', *Nature*, 364 (22 July 1993).

our behavioural patterns culture-based and so learned, no matter what they may have been in prehistory?

This objection might appear to have some weight. Edward Wilson concedes that since the development of agriculture 10,000 years ago almost all behavioural change has been culture-driven. (And it might be necessary to push the date for this innovation back as far as *c.* 30,000 years ago to the emergence of the advanced stone tool culture of the Cro-Magnons.) It is tempting to think, therefore, that we have slipped free from dependence on biologically determined behavioural traits.

The answer of sociobiology is that for several *million* years before the advent of a culture sufficiently advanced to respond rapidly to environmental pressures, our hominid ancestors lived as widely scattered bands of hunter-gatherers with stone tool cultures that were too primitive and static to be the driving force of behavioural change. (The Acheulean culture of *Homo erectus* and early *Homo sapiens* remained essentially unchanged over a wide geographical range for more than a million years.[3]) For *Homo habilis, Homo erectus*, the Neanderthals and early *Homo sapiens* behavioural change was essentially Darwinian – that is, traits were selected biologically, under environmental stress, from random genetic mutation.

Wilson argues that behavioural traits so developed over such an immense period of time were not simply made redundant by subsequent and comparatively recent (and rapid) culture-directed adaptation. Rather, the deeply ingrained *evolved* patterns of behaviour of our hunter-gatherer ancestors provided the foundation on which we have erected almost all the cultural elaborations we now refer to as civilization. He explains this by reference to the phenomenon of hypertrophy in evolutionary biology – the development to extremes of a structure already in existence. Examples he provides are the teeth of a baby elephant which elongate into tusks; the huge antlers of the male elk derived from the animal's cranial bones (*On Human Nature*).

Culture, Wilson believes, exhibits similar characteristics of hypertrophy, modern social behaviour consisting largely of 'hypertrophic outgrowths of the simpler features of human

---

[3] Richard G. Klein, *The Human Career: Human Biological and Cultural Origins* (University of Chicago Press, 1989).

nature joined together into an irregular mosaic'. In other words, the genetically determined behavioural patterns of our distant ancestors represent the deep structure of our behaviour now. Some of these 'outgrowths' are easy to recognize, such as incest taboos and 'the details of child care and kin classification which represent only slight alterations that have not yet concealed their Pleistocene origins'.

> Others, such as religion and class structure, are such gross transmutations that only the combined resources of anthropology and history can hope to trace their cultural phylogeny back to rudiments in the hunter-gatherer's repertory. (*On Human Nature*)

Behavioural hypertrophy is an intriguing hypothesis which may well explain a number of persistent behavioural traits in humans which are otherwise perplexing and apparently irrational. One is our species' predisposition for aggression which Wilson argues is best understood as an innate, genetically determined trait that evolved as a survival strategy over several million years among our hunter-gatherer ancestors. Modern forms of organized aggression are consequently hypertrophied outgrowths of this deep structure that are culturally determined. Seen in this light,

> . . . human aggression cannot be explained as either a dark-angelic flaw or a bestial instinct. Nor is it the pathological symptom of upbringing in a cruel environment. Human beings are strongly disposed to respond with unreasoning hatred to external threats and to escalate their hostility sufficiently to overwhelm the source of the threat by a respectably wide margin of safety.

The influence of this genetically determined deep structure of human behaviour may even extend to some of our profoundest intuitions about aesthetics. Several scientists, according to Wilson, have pointed out the remarkable similarity that exists between the parks and formal gardens to be found in many civilizations and the savannah environment where our hominid ancestors underwent crucial evolutionary development three million or more years ago. Examples are the *hortus conclusus*, the idealized walled garden of the Middle Ages, and the mansion with park of the eighteenth-century gentry. Each is a landscape dotted with trees but essentially open, with an element of order 'but less than geometric perfection'. Time and again we re-create this configuration and find it beautiful. As Wilson observes: 'Arcturian zoologists visiting this planet could make no sense of our morality and art until they reconstructed our genetic history'; adding, 'nor can we' (*Biophilia*, 1984).

It should now be clear that the programme sociobiology has set itself is extremely ambitious. If human social behaviour (no matter what hypertrophic cultural forms it may take today) is biological in its deep structure, that is, if it is based on *evolved* traits in the Darwinian sense, then we cannot understand what we really are until we understand that underlying structure from our species' prehistory and its convoluted pathways into the present.

Such understanding has a price, however – one which is exacted for every advance in science – and that is a realization of our species' marginality in the order of things. It is a realization which perhaps comes hardest from the neo-Darwinian synthesis. It is possible, at least, to see in the new physics a door left ajar for God and the pursuit of mystical experience. This is not the case with evolutionary biology which predicates, in Wilson's words, that 'no species, including our own, possesses a purpose beyond the imperatives created by its genetic history'. 'Species', he continues, 'may have vast potential for material and mental progress but they lack any immanent purpose or guidance from agents beyond their immediate environment or even an evolutionary goal toward which their molecular architecture automatically steers them.' Put starkly, 'The species [that is, the human species] lacks any goal external to its own biological nature' (*On Human Nature*).

Edward Wilson's response is to embrace this perception enthusiastically as a major advance in our search for an answer to the question 'What are we?' and as an opportunity to make informed choices about the direction humanity should take in the future based on thorough knowledge of the biological imperatives that have shaped us in the past. This is an eminently rational response and Wilson advocates it forcefully in *On Human Nature*. At the same time it is one which Wilson half-reluctantly admits we are very unlikely to take. Wilson's appeal is to reason, but though we are capable of reason individually, as a species we are driven by our emotions and the need to give our lives significant emotional validity. To put it another way, we have within us a need to be saved.

This need itself, I would suggest, is part of the biologically evolved deep structure of human nature, a product of that moment in evolutionary history when *Homo sapiens* or one of our ancestor species crossed the threshold of consciousness which gave us awareness of death, out of which developed the search for consolation in religion. The need is still there for our condition has not changed, but it is not and cannot be satisfied within the neo-Darwinian frame of reference. Hence we have what Wilson calls 'the enduring paradox of religion' in our age, which is 'that so much of its substance is demonstrably false, yet it remains a driving-force in all societies'. He adds: 'Men would rather believe than know, have the void as purpose, as Nietzsche said, than be void of purpose' (*Sociobiology*).

This paradox has driven a deep wedge into modern civilization, for while we can no longer survive in the developed nations without science neither can we bear to live, for the most part, with its philosophical implications. Wilson quotes an American Gallup poll from 1977 which showed that in one of the scientifically most advanced nations on Earth, 94 per cent of the population believed in God in some form or other while 31 per cent had experienced 'a moment of sudden religious insight or awakening, their brush with the epiphany'. As Wilson observes, 'Our schizophrenic societies progress by knowledge but survive on inspiration derived from the very beliefs which that knowledge erodes' (*On Human Nature*).

And here we have a crux. There are those, and some scientists among them, who argue that science and religion are not the irreconcilable opposites that they seem and that Wilson claims. Rather they are different modes of perception operating in different domains, each equally valid in its own domain – that is, the material universe which is open to science's rational form of inquiry involving verifiable evidence; and that-which-is-beyond, the ineffable, which by definition can never be the proper subject of such investigation.

Personally, I have never found this argument convincing.

Through its myths religion has always staked a claim to the interpretation of the material world and for this reason alone Christianity has fought a rearguard action against science in Europe and America for several centuries. The 'different domain' argument really depends on one branch of science, the new physics, which appears to give religion a let out. To quote Wilson again:

> As science proceeds to dismantle the ancient mythic stories one by one, theology retreats to the final redoubt from which it can never be driven. This is the idea of God in the creation myth: God as will, the cause of existence, and the agent who generated all of the energy in the original fireball and set the natural laws by which the universe evolved. So long as the redoubt exists, theology can slip out through its portals and make occasional sallies into the real world. Whenever other philosophers let their guard down, deists can, in the manner of process theology, postulate a pervasive transcendental will. They can even hypothesize miracles. (*On Human Nature*)

The real opposition, as this suggests, is not so much between religion and science as such but between religion and evolutionary biology, as fundamentalist Christians in America were quick to perceive. For a central tenet of Christianity, that there is a divine purpose to life on Earth, is negated by a central tenet of the Darwinian interpretation of nature, that life on Earth has had no purpose in its nearly four thousand million years of existence beyond, in Wilson's words, 'the imperatives created by its genetic history'. If this is so there is no teleology in nature and there can be no divine purpose: life evolves without direction through environmental pressure exerted on the random mutation of genes. One position cancels the other out, they cannot both be right, a fact which no doubt explains the aggressive campaign by fundamentalists to promote the pseudo-biology Creationism side-by-side with evolutionary biology in America's schools, as well as the equally aggressive atheism of neo-Darwinists such as Richard Dawkins and Edward O. Wilson.

Wilson is of course aware of the great psychological crisis caused by the steady erosion of religious myths in the face of the advance of science. 'The price of these failures has been a loss of moral consensus, a greater sense of helplessness about the human condition and a shrinking back toward the self and the immediate future' (*On Human Nature*). And his response is typically bold in its attempt to seek a resolution in scientific materialism itself which, with its core, 'the evolutionary epic', is, he argues, in essence a great mythopoeic vision. In *On Human Nature* he presents its 'minimum claims':

> . . . that the laws of the physical sciences are consistent with those of the biological and social sciences and can be linked in chains of causal explanation; that life and mind have a physical basis; that the world as we know it has evolved from earlier worlds obedient to the same laws, and that the visible universe today is everywhere subject to these materialist explanations.

This statement is mythopoeic in that while it presents a coherent view of the universe and our species' place in it, and while aspects of the 'epic' can be strengthened through further research, none the less 'its most sweeping assertions cannot be proved with finality'. In other words, scientific materialism too demands an act of faith. The evolutionary epic is nevertheless, he claims, 'probably the best myth we will ever have'.

I believe this is true. But as a myth to succeed the myths of religion it has a flaw which relates directly to a fundamental need of our species which, ironically enough, sociobiology would trace back to our evolved biological nature. It is a flaw which Wilson chooses to discount in his commitment to reason, but it is likely to be fatal to his enterprise. For the evolutionary epic only satisfies one function of myth, which is to provide a coherent and inclusive explanation of natural phenomena. It does not and cannot satisfy the other, which is to place humanity within that explanation in such a way that our life is given meaning.

Wilson is of course *aware* of this. Scientific materialism will, he believes, one day make theology redundant. Sociobiology has already made a start by attempting to explore 'the biological sources of religious emotional strength'. But scientific materialism lacks religion's 'primal source of power' and can never draw on it because, unlike religion, its appeal is not to the emotions but to reason. Thus 'the evolutionary epic denies immortality to the individual and divine privilege to the society, and it suggests only an existential meaning for the human species' – because this is the rational deduction to be made from the evidence. Hence under the dispensation of scientific materialism, 'humanists will never enjoy the hot pleasures of spiritual conversion and self-surrender; scientists cannot in all honesty serve as priests'.

Wilson, however, appears to believe that this does not matter, that once the new synthesis of sociobiology with the social sciences and the humanities has been achieved, we will, for example, be able to create a new ethics based on a rational assessment of our fundamental biological nature.

But here the whole sociobiological enterprise runs out in the sands. One of its basic tenets, as we have seen, is that the deep structure of human social behaviour is evolved, no matter the hypertrophic forms it may be given through culture. How then can we make rational choices among aspects of our behaviour, selecting some and rejecting others in order to control our future, as Wilson advocates, if the deep-structure behavioural forms are genetically inherited? We might make conscious efforts to repress some of the less desirable behavioural patterns or to divert them into harmless channels. But even if we go along with the fantasies of the eugenicists it is unlikely that we can eradicate them. The ability to reason must have evolved quite late in the history of the genus Homo. At our deepest level we have always been and remain emotional beings, and not only do the emotions make strong demands on us for fulfilment which are hard to resist, they are the prime movers in our will to be. Moreover, because the emotions are inherently chaotic, they determine the basic pattern of our lives and social interactions, which can at best be described as provisional and muddled.

For these reasons, as Wilson rightly says at one point, 'the predisposition to religious belief is the most complex and powerful force in the human mind and in all probability an ineradicable part of human nature' (*On Human Nature*). In Wilson's view, those who succumb sacrifice reason and truth to their emotional needs. I believe this to be correct. But what of those who subordinate such needs to reason? I cannot believe in Wilson's vision of a new rational order for humankind and my reasons are grounded in the fundamental tenets of his own theory.

'The dry light of reason is ever the best,' wrote Francis Bacon in the seventeenth century. Yet as we gaze on what that light appears to reveal we seem not so much like the inhabitants of Edward Wilson's rational eugenic world, but more and more like the space-pilots of Aniara in Harry Martinson's epic poem. They are 'fatalists of the new kind' who could only have been formed by the vast emptiness of deep space. For them

> ... döden ingår bara helt naturligt
> i deras schema som en klar konstant.

> ... death is included quite naturally
> as an obvious constant in their scheme of things.

Yet as the ship heads year after year deeper into space away from Earth, they too 'look down from terror's precipice'. At such times does the narrator catch them out and see into their minds:

> I någon obevakat ögonblik, men välbevakat
> av mig som läser deras anletsdrag
> kan sorgen lysa som ett fosforsken
> ur deras spanarögon.

> In an unguarded moment, but closely observed
> by me, who read their features,
> sorrow can glitter like a phosphorous shine
> from their searching eyes.

5

The candle in the window

Heddiw'r bore cefais hyd i'r flwyddyn newydd-anedig ar garreg fy nrws yn crefu am gael croeso i'r tŷ. Petrusais ennyd gan fod ofn arnaf beth a ddôi i'w chanlyn. Ond dal i ymbil a wnaeth hyd nes y'i codais, nid o dosturi ond oherwydd y bu rhaid.

This morning I found the new-born year on my doorstep begging to be welcomed into the house. I hesitated a moment because I was afraid of what might come in its train. But it went on pleading, until I picked it up, not out of pity, but out of necessity.

So begins *Blwyddyn yn Llŷn* (A Year in Llŷn) by R. S. Thomas. It is a journal, divided into twelve chapters, one for each month of the year, though it is not the journal of any particular year, for at one point he refers to the murder of Olof Palme (1986) as happening 'yesterday', while entries for November and December discuss the collapse of Communist régimes in Eastern Europe (1989). It is in fact a distillation of many years lived in Llŷn, and is both a celebration of the peninsula and a showing forth of the feelings, thoughts and experience of what he calls at the end 'dyn cyffredin', an ordinary man.

That opening paragraph is far from ordinary, however, and if *Blwyddyn yn Llŷn* reminds me of anything it is Coleridge's *Notebooks*. In each there is the sense of a powerful mind unifying the fragments of a life, as that mind probes the nature of reality and what it is to be human, both as a general phenomenon, and as the 'I' living out its imperfect existence.

The journal, as might be expected, covers some familiar R. S. Thomas territory: the state of the language, of Wales, English mass culture, and so on. It also reveals his wry humour, something which is more evident in his conversation than in his writing. Returning by train to Pwllheli, he hears the sound of a brass band as the train draws into the station. 'Mae Pwllheli wedi troi allan o'r diwedd,' he half-jokes to himself, 'i roi gwir groeso i fardd!' (Pwllheli has turned out at last to give a true welcome to a poet!) But as he leaves his carriage, he finds that Siôn Corn (Santa Claus) was also on board and that the town band and the hundreds of cheering children and parents are for him. Fair enough, the poet thinks, 'fedra i ddim cystadlu â Siôn Corn' (I can't compete with Siôn Corn).

Blwyddyn yn Llŷn is also of course an expression of his life-long absorption in nature, especially the sea and birds. In retrospect, he has come to view his years in Manafon and Eglwys-fach as a protracted exile from the sea, which stirred his imagination so much as a child. It is a constant backdrop of sight and sound in the journal entries. Then there are the birds, the pleasure of the unexpected as a tree-creeper flashes past to clamp itself to a nearby tree 'a dechrau hercian ar ei ffordd i fyny fel clocwaith' (and begin to hop its way up like clockwork) – a comparison which captures exactly the short, jerky, wound-up movements of the bird climbing the vertical trunk of a tree.

Such moments (always, it seems, experienced alone) come close at times to the mystical, or at least to something elusive and timeless which is different from ordinary experience. He describes how once he stood in the middle of a wood where everything was so still he could hear the distant murmur of the sea. Standing so still himself, it is almost as if he enters the wood and becomes part of it. Suddenly, he is aware of a flock of goldcrests, those tiny restless birds, flitting towards him through the trees. The branches above his head are full of them, so close he can see their eyes 'fel hadau'r mwyar duon' (like blackberry seeds). It is almost as if one of them must perch on him, but gradually the flock moves on and he is left alone, 'a dim ond pelydrau'r haul i'm hatgoffa o aur eu cribau' (and only the sun's rays to remind me of the gold of their crests). It is, as he says, an example of how birds, and nature itself, will accept you if you cultivate patience to show that there is no harm in you ('ond i chi fagu digon o amynedd i brofi iddynt nad oes dim drwg ynoch').[1]

Blwyddyn yn Llŷn is crowded with observations like these which reveal a great delight in life. Why, then, that initial hesitation, reluctance even, to welcome the New Year which is described in the journal's memorable opening paragraph? It certainly doesn't come from distaste for life, but it does reveal a complex attitude to it. Twice in the journal he reflects on Yeats's saying that if he had the chance he would gladly live life over again. Would R. S. Thomas say the same? He has thought about it many a time, and has doubts. 'Ac eto mae'r llais yn fy ymyl yn sibrwd: wrth gwrs dy fod yn barod.' (And yet the voice beside me whispers: of course you're willing.)

This comes at the end of a paragraph which reveals the intricate (and Coleridgean) interplay of ideas, emotion and experience which is characteristic of the journal. It begins with him reading Nietzsche and reflecting on the philosopher's dictum that 'dim ond fel ffenomen esthetig y gellir cyfiawnhau bywyd yn dragwyddol' (life without end can only be justified as an aesthetic phenomenon). R. S. Thomas has felt the truth of this many a time, 'wrth syllu ar harddwch amhersonol didostur natur' (from gazing on the impersonal, pitiless beauty of nature). He thinks of his admiration for the beauty of birds of prey that are none the less killers, and of a stoat he saw that day: 'llofrudd hardd arall, ond yn symud mor heini dros y ddaear, mor ysgafn â phluen' (another beautiful murderer, but moving so nimbly across the earth, light as a feather). After watching it for a while, he had glanced up and seen Ynys Gybi in the distance in sunlight, 'a daeth yr un hen hiraeth amhosibl amdani, nid fel y mae hi, ond fel yr oedd. Bûm unwaith yn hogyn yno. Pe cawn dewis!' (and I experienced the same impossible old longing for it, not as it is, but as it was. I was a lad there once. If I had the choice!) And it is this which leads to his reflection on Yeats's self-confident boast; because for R. S. Thomas it is not so simple. 'Wrth roi geiriau i'r posibilrwydd, rwy'n dechrau simsanu' (As I put the possibility into words, I begin to waver).

Like all of us, R. S. Thomas experiences time in two ways, as a cycle, best seen in the recurrence of the seasons, and as a line,

---

[1] The incident is the source of the poem 'A Thicket in Lleyn' in *Experimenting with an Amen* (Macmillan, 1986).

time's arrow which takes us relentlessly from birth to death.[2] His hesitation at welcoming the New Year and at the thought of reliving his life, comes, it seems to me, from an acute awareness of this dual aspect of time. For in the recurrence of the seasons, in the annual migration of the birds, he finds reasons for joy. To be alive to relive the beauty of the raptor, or the stoat. But living life again would also submit him to time's arrow, to the linear certainty of ageing, death and (likely) annihilation. 'Mae'r ifanc yn ei dderbyn ac yn dweud Amen, yn rhinwedd eu hoen a'u bywiogrwydd' (The young accept it and say Amen, by virtue of their vigour and vitality). But what of the old?

R. S. Thomas does not use these images of time's cycle and time's arrow himself, but his inherent recognition of this dual and conflicting function of time in our lives provides a deep structure for the experiences recorded in the journal.

This is seen most clearly in some remarkable entries about women. An entry for February begins, 'Heddiw gwelais hi eto ar ôl misoedd o absenoldeb' (Today I saw her again after months of absence). A car had passed him in the street without him paying too much attention, until suddenly it strikes him who was driving. He walks on, and then catches a glimpse of her further down the street. It leads to a kind of agonizing. Hers is the most beautiful face he has seen since his wife was young. He wants to know who she is, and yet at the same time he realizes that it is best not to know, to keep her at a distance. 'Gadawer iddi gadw'i dieithrwch, ac i finnau, fel Dante gyda'i Beatrice, gael cip arni o dro i dro, fel y caf yfed am foment o'i harddwch tan y tro nesaf' (Let her keep her strangeness, and let me glimpse her now and then, like Dante his Beatrice, so that I can drink from her beauty for a moment until the next time). He knows that if he pointed her out to others they would not understand his feelings, for her beauty is tinged with sorrow as one who suffers, and there are few in the world who would consider that a good thing. But his wife would understand because she is an artist, 'ac ni bydd arlunydd na bardd yn gweld fel mae eraill yn gweld' (and neither artist nor poet sees as others see).

The beauty of the suffering face is like the beauty of pitiless

[2] See Stephen Jay Gould, *Time's Arrow, Time's Cycle* (1987; Penguin, 1988).

nature. It is distanced from him, belonging to time's cycle in the sense that it is ever-recurring, as the reference to Dante's Beatrice suggests. Like nature, it is the source of a particular kind of artistic creativity. However, there is a difference. Nature's impersonality can never be violated by the observer; but the beauty of the suffering face? To get to know her would be to draw her into the world of linear time of ageing and death, which the poet, an ordinary man walking along the street, inhabits.

In this instance, it is easy to keep that necessary distance. But it is not always so. Out birdwatching one day in October, he looks across at Y Rhiw and thinks of the evening before, when a young woman (he does not say who) escorted him to the lane, 'mor ifanc ac mor ddel nes ei bod hi'n anodd peidio â rhoi cusan iddi' (so young and so pretty that it was hard to refrain from giving her a kiss). Yet now, in the light of day, he is glad he resisted the temptation. For he sees himself, not as he feels within, but as others see him from without, an ageing man. How many would understand the true nature of such a kiss?

> Faint o bobl sy'n deall tristwch hen ŵr ar adegau? Daw'r geiriau difeddwl: 'yr hen ffŵl gwirion' neu 'yr hen ŵr budr' yn rhy rwydd i'r tafod. Tra byddaf byw daliaf i deimlo apêl genod ifanc, del. Rydw i'n cofio fy nhad ar ei wely angau yn yr ysbyty yn ymbil â'i lygaid am i'r genod wenu arno wrth fynd heibio iddo'n ddi-hid . . .

> How many people understand the sadness of an old man at times? Thoughtless words come easily to the tongue: 'the silly old fool' or 'the dirty old man'. So long as I live, I'll continue to feel the attraction of pretty young girls. I remember my father as he lay on his deathbed in hospital entreating the girls with his eyes to smile at him as they went heedlessly by . . .

These incidents are paradoxical. A certain kind of suffering beauty must be kept at a distance in order for it to remain inviolate; just as a certain kind of tenderness (the bestowal of a kiss in recognition of a girl's loveliness) must be repressed, lest it be misunderstood. Yet in the moment with the goldcrests in the wood, it is as if he had merged into the natural world, had not only become one with it in spirit, but literally a part of its impersonality and its beauty. As he says in the poem 'A Thicket in Lleyn':

> They would have perched
> on me, had I had nourishment
> in my fissures.

As he looks at Y Rhiw and thinks of the girl in the lane the previous evening, he remembers how at Manafon he often climbed the hill behind the Rectory 'ac wrth edrych i lawr a gweld y pentref mor fach, cael pethau i berspectif' (and on looking down and seeing the village so tiny, get things in perspective).

Yet the poet must come down from the hill, emerge from the timeless moment in the wood, and become an ordinary man again. And that is why human beauty, when it enters your life, must be tinged with sorrow, for what at a distance may seem unchanged, or at least ever-recurring in time's cycle, like the face of Beatrice, is different when it touches you and moves with you in linear time towards death.

In an entry for September, he mentions that his wife is in hospital and so some friends have invited him to supper:

Dychwelais i dŷ heb dân, heb gannwyll. Cysgodion o'r hyn a ddaw? Mae'r wraig yn hŷn na mi. Os digwydd fel yna, bydd yn anodd dysgu dychwelyd i dŷ lle na fydd golau yn y ffenestr. Heno, yn lle ymhyfrydu yn swn y môr odanaf, fe'i clywais yn ddigon garw a digysur am unwaith.

I returned to a house without a fire, without a candle. Shades of what is to come? My wife is older than me. If it turns out that way, it will be hard to get used to returning to a house where there is no light in the window. Tonight, instead of delighting in the sound of the sea below, I heard it as something harsh and comfortless, for once.

On New Year's Eve, R. S. Thomas had placed a candle in the window 'i ddangos i ba ysbryd bynnag oedd ar goll yn y gwyll fod yna groeso iddo yma' (to show any spirit lost in the darkness that there was a welcome here). Now, for just a moment, he is that spirit in the dark in need of a welcoming light. On New Year's Eve he had set the candle in the window for all humanity, and himself.

~

These incidents are shafts of light cast by a complex mind upon itself; the mind of someone who is by nature a solitary, yet who has turned more and more to autobiography, especially in Welsh, as if from a need to show himself forth more directly; the mind daring itself to make itself more vulnerable.

At the same time the poet has taken on an increasingly public role which *has* made him vulnerable, to the vilification and even hatred of those with no liking for unpalatable truths. The two developments are not unrelated, and they make *Blwyddyn yn Llŷn* both an intensely personal and a highly politicized book. (For R. S. Thomas has always been one of our most political poets, though his politics has been forged out of his own thinking rather than the latest trend.)

For this reason alone, his views have not been popular. But, to some extent, they have also been misunderstood at a much more fundamental level than mere agreement or disagreement with a particular agenda. For R. S. Thomas is a political man in the Romantic sense: someone who thinks of society in absolute terms of an ideal, against which the inadequacies of the real are to be measured. *Blwyddyn yn Llŷn*, like *Neb* and *Pe Medrwn yr Iaith*, is full of concern for, and ideas about, Welsh society, full of imaginings as to what it would be like to live in a rounded, rather than a fragmented Welsh (meaning for him, of course, Welsh-language) culture.

But how that ideal might be approached, or how we might shore up its fragments in the world of *Realpolitik* is another matter. In his personal life he has worked as a language and CND activist, but in his writings, there is a gap which at times seems unbridgeable between the ideal and the real. This makes it easy for the unsympathetic to dismiss his political statements as hot air, or worse. But society needs strong figures whose politics are absolute, not relative – who will not budge because the times are against them. It is too easy to move 'with the times' in a world where shifts and evasions and fudgings are taken for granted.

Yet, it still might be asked, what exactly are R. S. Thomas's politics? The 'fascist' smear hardly accords with someone who opposed the poll tax and privatization on the grounds of their evident social injustice, nor with the CND campaigner. But he is no socialist either and the journal provides plenty of evidence for his Saunders Lewis-like distaste for urban mass culture. Reflecting on tourism in Llŷn, he says that people have told him that the peninsula attracted a more cultured type of tourist years ago. But now when he goes to Pwllheli there is always some Tom, Dick or Harry strolling in the street 'neu'n eistedd yn eu cerbydau gyda phapur newydd rhyngddynt a'r golygfeydd, gan lladd amser tan amser agor y tafarnau neu ddechrau adloniant yr hwyr yn Butlins' (or sitting in their cars with a newspaper between themselves and the view, killing time before opening time at the pubs or the evening's entertainment begins at Butlins). This sounds, as he says, snobbish ('Mae hyn yn swnio'n snobyddlyd, mi wn . . .'), but it has to be set against another passage in the journal.

One day he is out in the countryside enjoying the stillness of early spring. Suddenly, the song of the birds is overwhelmed by the engine-roar of low-flying fighters ('negeseuwyr angau', messengers of death). But a voice within asks, who is he to challenge the authority of the State, which has decided that these machines are necessary as a means of keeping peace. 'O ie,' he answers cynically:

Clywsom hyn o'r blaen dros y blynyddoedd. Mi wn pwy ydi'r wladwriaeth 'ma – clic o bobl uchelgeisiol a ddarbwyllodd eu hetholaethau i lyncu'u propaganda, ac wedi'u hethol, yn lle cynrychioli buddiannau'u hetholwyr, cynrychioli'r gwanc a'r ariangarwch a'r grym sydd ynghlwm wrthynt. Pa ddiddordeb sydd gan rhain ym myd natur a'i hen drefn ryfeddol? Ond rydym ni mewn awdurdod i'ch gwarchod rhag y gelyn, meddant. Gyfeillion, does arnaf ddim eisiau i chi ddweud pwy ydi'r gelyn. Chi ydi o, cyn belled â'ch bod yn barod i lygru'r ddaear a'r amgylchedd er eich budd chi.

We've heard this before over the years. I know who this State is – a clique of ambitious people who persuaded the electorate to swallow their propaganda, and on being elected, instead of representing the welfare of the voters, represent the greed and avarice and power which they have in common. What interest do these have in nature and its ancient and wonderful order? But we're in authority to protect you from the enemy, they say. Friends, I don't need you to tell me who the enemy is. It's you, inasmuch as you are prepared to contaminate the earth and the environment for your own profit.

He realizes that anyone who topples such a power structure would in turn become the enemy, 'since the same kind of man seeks political and financial power in any country'. So what is the answer? Self-government, in the strict sense of the word. 'Nid oes arna i eisiau neb i'm llywodraethu. Dyna wir ystyr hunan-lywodraeth, eich bod yn gallu'ch disgyblu'ch hun.' (I don't need anyone to govern me. That's the true meaning of self-government, that you can discipline yourself.) All that is needed is a body of people to organize social and political matters and a police force in its true meaning (*heddlu: hedd + llu* = peace-force) to prevent anyone from overthrowing a just society and to protect the weak.

This is a form of anarcho-syndicalism, which if it were to have a chance of success, would have to take place in communities organized on a small scale. Set here against the war machines of the power-state, it is clear that R. S. Thomas does not imagine it to be an attainable goal in the world in which we live. Rather, it is a one-man declaration of independence, an affirmation of individuality in a mass society which discourages individualism with its slogans, propaganda and consumerism.

Those who are like-minded may join together to serve a cause. So the poet is a member of CND and Cyfeillion Llŷn (The Friends of Llŷn). But such groups have little impact on society at large. The journal is full of entries about poor attendance at meetings, the indifference of the public, the feeling of dejection as his CND branch meets after ten years of largely fruitless campaigning in Llŷn.

And this brings us back to his 'snobbish' comments on the English working-class holiday-makers: '. . . ychydig o gydymdeimlad sydd gennyf, am mai dyma'r bobl wrth eu miliynau sy'n prysur ladd y Gymraeg, a'r Cymry'n eu croesawu am fod ganddynt bres. Pryd mae digon yn ddigon, ys gwn i?' (. . . I have little sympathy with them, because these are the people in their millions who are busily killing off Welsh, and the Welsh welcoming them because they have money. When is enough enough, I'd like to know?)

This is the familiar R. S. Thomas pincer attack on English mass society and those among the Welsh who embrace it at the expense of their own language and culture, and it is stated here in a typically blunt and uncompromising way. Such statements are bound to cause offence, yet underlying them is a truth which ought to be evident to any Welsh man or woman who thinks about it, no matter how tragic and self-divisive such realization might be. In October, he was reading George Steiner's *After Babel*, which stresses the unique role of language in the shaping of a nation. He comments in frustration, 'Pam o pam na fydd y Cymro cyffredin yn sylweddoli bod y genedl yn brwydro am ei heinioes?' (Why, oh why, can't the average Welshman realize that the nation is fighting for its life?) And he goes on: 'A ydi'r Sais-Cymro sy'n honni ei fod cystal Cymro â ni yn sylweddoli na fedr hyd yn oed deimlo'n Gymro heb syrthio'n ôl ar y gorffennol Cymraeg? Ond brwydr yr iaith heddiw ydi brwydr dros dyfodol i'r genedl.' (Does the Anglicized Welshman who declares he's just as Welsh as we are, realize that you can't even feel Welsh without recourse to the Welsh [i.e. Welsh-language] past? The only fight for the future of the nation today is the fight for the language.)

And in November, reflecting on events in Eastern Europe, he thinks: 'Un brif iaith oedd gan y gwledydd hyn yn Ewrob, eu hiaith genedlaethol, er eu bod dan ormes mewn cyfeiriadau eraill. Felly ni chollasant mo'u hunanymwybyddiaeth genedl-aethol' (These countries in Europe had one main language, their national language, even though they were oppressed in other ways. So they did not lose their national self-consciousness).

The truth of this seems obvious, as does its relevance to Wales. Had Russia been capable of a programme of Russification throughout Poland, so that Russian, rather than Polish, became the majority language, there can be no question but that Polish awareness of itself as a nation, and its willingness to resist, would have been severely weakened if not eradicated. For, as he implies, language is the key to the past, and a knowledge of the past is the key to a nation's self-awareness, and hence its ability to project itself into the future.

This would be self-evident to a Pole – or to a Swede or a Finn, or to that nation even smaller than the Welsh-speaking Welsh, the Icelanders. But at home, this is not the case, and plain speaking has earned R. S. Thomas much hatred. The majority do not like being told: 'Mae ein harweinwyr bondigrybwyll ni'n wleidyddol naïf neu'n anonest, os credant y gallwn gadw'n hunaniaeth tra'n siarad Saesneg fel ein prif iaith a gwneud cyfeillion mynwesol o'r Saeson' (Our leaders are indeed politically naïve or dishonest if they believe we can maintain our identity while speaking English as our main language and making bosom friends of the English). But then, Wales is not Poland, or Sweden, or Finland, or Iceland. Wales has been much too successfully infiltrated by the English and English mass culture for that, so that it is easier for our politicians to be dishonest or naïve, or to play possum, for that is essentially what the majority of the people of Wales want.

Yet it may be asked, against R. S. Thomas, what right has he to pronounce on behalf of Welsh-speaking Wales? He was thirty before he began to learn the language, and that must always make him, in important ways, an outsider. Perhaps he speaks with the fervour of the convert, which can seem embarrassing to the insider. I have heard it said by Welsh-speakers: 'Oh, R. S. Thomas, he doesn't understand the Welsh.' Perhaps. But perhaps, as sometimes happens with outsiders, his ambiguous position in Welsh society allows him to see more clearly (and too clearly for some) what is happening to the nation. He knows that there are those in Llŷn who think he is a crank or worse, but that is the fate of the individual who thinks for himself and dares express his thoughts. As we all become more processed in a mass society, we must toe the line, or be punished.

In such a world, what can the individual do? It may not be much, but R. S. Thomas's answer is the politics of resistance, the anarchist opposition of one. In a store in Bangor, a Welsh-speaking salesgirl directs him to a man at another counter. '"Cymro, ie?" "No,"' the man replies in English, 'gan sgwario'i ysgwyddau, fel petae dan warchae' (squaring his shoulders, as if under siege). All right, the poet thinks, 'Tipyn o'u ffisig eu hunain i'r Saeson o hyn allan' (A bit of their own medicine for the English from now on). So now, when he is stopped by some tourist in Llŷn asking directions, he just says 'Dim Saesneg', or shrugs his shoulders and shakes his head 'fel un heb fod yn llawn llathen' (like someone who's not all there).

There are many such anecdotes in *Blwyddyn yn Llŷn*, some of them bitter, some amusing. They are the inevitable consequences of trying to live out that imagined, ideal life, in a Wales which is fragmenting. Such things would not be happening to him, and his bitterness would not be such a burden, if he lived in Sweden or Iceland. Yet, as he places a candle in the window at the end of another year, at the close of this journal, it is hard not to feel that R. S. Thomas has lived as full a Welsh life as perhaps is possible under present conditions, and that he has done so because of his vision and his refusal to compromise it.

An entry for October encapsulates in a moving way what that vision means to him, and how great would be its loss:

Neithiwr breuddwydais yr un hen freuddwyd a fod yn dychwelyd mor aml: minnau'n ôl ym Manafon, wedi gorfod gadael Llŷn i ailafael ynddi fel Rheithor Manafon. Y tristwch o feddwl fy mod wedi cefnu ar y Gymraeg a'm cyfeillion oll, a rhyw fodloni pŵl ar bethau'n cymryd eu lle; dim môr, dim harddwch Llŷn, dim bwthyn lle mae Cymry wedi byw a gweithio dros y canrifoedd; dim adar ymfudol yn mynd heibio yn y gwanwyn a'r hydref. Ond rhyw deimlad torcalonnus fy mod wedi llosgi pont ac wedi cymryd cam di-droi'n ôl. A'r llawenydd wedyn wrth ddeffro a sylweddoli'n ara deg fy mod yn Llŷn wedi'r cyfan, yn y lle mae arna' i eisiau bod. Dirgel ffyrdd y dyn tu mewn imi, ond mor ddychrynllyd o real!

Last night I dreamed the same old dream, which returns so often; I was back in Manafon, having been obliged to leave Llŷn to become Rector of Manafon again. The sadness at the thought of turning my back on Welsh and all my friends, and a kind of dull acceptance of things in their place; no sea, none of Llŷn's beauty; no cottage where Welsh people have lived and worked for centuries; no migrant birds in spring and autumn. But a heart-breaking feeling that I'd burnt my bridges and taken a step from which there was no turning back. And the joy afterwards on waking and realizing gradually that I was in Llŷn after all, in the place where I want to be. Secret paths of the man within, but how frighteningly real!

6

The age of the arthropods

In *Wonderful Life*,[1] Stephen Jay Gould makes available to the non-specialist the results of a revolution in palaeontology. It concerns the significance of fossils in a bed of Cambrian shale about 530 million years old, high in the Canadian Rockies, known as the Burgess Shale. The importance of these fossils has been recognized since they were discovered by the American palaeontologist Charles Doolittle Walcott in 1909. For obvious reasons, the soft parts of animals are rarely preserved in the process of fossilization, but in the Burgess Shale they are, and this has enabled palaeontologists to reconstruct in fine detail the anatomy of animals that existed just after the Cambrian 'explosion': a critical period about 570 million years ago when (for reasons which are still not well understood) anatomically complex multicellular organisms appear to have burst upon the Cambrian seas for the first time. It is as if, in the Burgess Shale, we are given a bathysphere let down into that distant period, from the windows of which we can observe the Earth's earliest complex creatures.

However, the view from a window is determined, in part, by what we expect to see, and Charles Walcott brought to his interpretation of the Burgess Shale fossils a conceptual framework which led him badly astray. It was only in the 1970s after a systematic redescription of the fossils was undertaken by

[1] *Wonderful Life: The Burgess Shale and the Nature of History* (Hutchinson Radius, 1990).

Harry Whittington and a group of Cambridge palaeontologists, that their real significance began to come clear.

Wonderful Life is both an account of Whittington's redescription and an explanation of why Walcott made the mistakes in interpretation that he did. But it is not merely of interest to the amateur palaeontologist or historian of science. For as Stephen Jay Gould explains in this magnificently documented study, the Burgess Shale fossils have major implications for the history of evolution and for the way in which we perceive ourselves. The Burgess revisions have in fact 'overturned something old and central to our culture' and cannot be ignored.

What this something is is belief in the centrality of our species, and of human consciousness, in the order of nature. Intellectually, Darwinism might be thought to have dispelled this belief a century ago, but in practice evolutionary theory came to be interpreted by scientists like Walcott in such a way that it seemed to confirm human centrality rather than negate it. For Walcott was a Christian as well as a conservative Darwinist and his beliefs created what Stephen Jay Gould calls an 'ideological constraint' on his scientific interpretation of evidence.

As a result, Walcott interpreted evolution as a 'progressive' force, something which is negated by the logic of the process of natural selection (though according to Gould, Darwin himself never entirely rid his thinking of the idea). Thus Walcott was able to consider himself a Darwinist while, in Gould's words, 'expressing by this stated allegiance his strong conviction that natural selection assured the survival of superior organisms and progressive improvement of life on a predictable pathway to consciousness'.

Evolution, in this view, leads by inevitable process, involving the extinction of the unfit, to *us*. And progressionism does not end there. Like others of his time, Walcott made no sharp distinction between biological evolution and social evolution among human beings. Walcott's argument is paraphrased by Gould: 'We mount in an unbroken climb through the ranks of organisms, and continue directly upward with the linear improvement of human technology.'

This notion is so powerful and attractive (though it has been abandoned by science) that it has come to underpin our habitual perceptions of ourselves and the world. In fact, most of us probably consider it a *fact* rather than an idea. Almost, it is too convenient to give up. For it bestows centrality and inevitability on the evolution of human consciousness which is acceptable to the secular mind, while to the religious it can (with a little adjustment) seem like a proof of the benevolence of God:

> It is a sublime conception of God which is furnished by science, and one wholly consonant with the highest ideals of religion, when it represents Him as revealing Himself through countless ages in the development of the earth as an abode for man and in the age-long inbreathing of life into its constituent matter, culminating in man with his spiritual nature and all his God-like power.
>
> (Walcott, quoted by Gould)

As Stephen Jay Gould shows in the important first chapter of *Wonderful Life*, this idea of evolution-as-progress is perpetuated by a cluster of very powerful images. One is of a ladder, with species mounting the rungs in a progressional series culminating in man. A more complex image is based on what Gould calls 'the cone of increasing diversity', usually pictured as a branching tree. According to this model, 'Life begins with the restricted and simple, and progresses ever upward to more and more and, by implication, better and better.'

Gould points out that in science such images are meant to be read literally: 'up and down should record only younger and older in geological time.' But such is the symbolic power of these ascending images that we can almost not help ourselves reading into them a system of values. So, 'we also read upward movement as simple to complex, or primitive to advanced.' In this way, 'Placement in time is conflated with judgment of worth.'

Such progressionist ideas led to Walcott's misreading of the Burgess Shale, his 'shoehorning' (Gould's term) of its creatures into a few phyla[2] based on the assumption that they represented older and therefore simpler examples of more recent and more successful species within the same phyla. There is a great diversity of species in the modern era, yet they are modelled on a very few body plans. The immense variety within the phylum

---

[2] I.e. major divisions of the animal kingdom based on fundamental differences in body plan.

Arthropoda, for instance, which includes the insects, spiders, crustacea and (the extinct) trilobites, is based on a single body plan. Knowing this, Walcott identified the Burgess Shale fossils that he examined as antecedents of creatures within modern phyla – he 'shoehorned' them in accordance with his belief in the cone of increasing diversity. But the re-examination of the fossils by Harry Whittington and his colleagues reveals something quite different – creatures exhibiting at least twenty-five different body plans, including 'eight anatomical designs that do not fit into any known animal phylum' (and the examination of the Burgess fossils is nowhere near complete).

The implication for the history of life and the meaning of our own species is immense, for although there are far more *species* today, 'The Burgess Shale includes a range of disparity in anatomical design never again equalled, and not matched by all the creatures in all the world's oceans.' The Cambrian explosion in fact seems to have released an extraordinary potential for genetic diversity. So, among the arthropods, characteristics which in later times became established features of particular groups were freely interchangeable for all kinds of species experiments. What is more, the structure of some of the exotic creatures of the Burgess Shale suggests that this potential may have applied *across* the boundaries of phyla.

However, this period of genetic experimentation on the grand scale was followed rapidly (in geological terms) by extinctions which wiped out the majority of body plans generated in the Cambrian explosion. For reasons that are not understood, it appears to have been a unique phase in the history of life. Later mass extinctions, such as the one which occurred at the juncture of the Permian and Triassic periods about 225 million years ago, 'may have wiped out 96 per cent or more of all marine species – yet the Burgess phenomenon of explosive disparity never occurred again. Life did rediversify quickly after the Permian extinction, but no new phyla arose; the recolonizers of a depleted earth all remained within the strictures of previous anatomical designs.' One theory, according to Gould, is that genetic systems 'age' and become more resistant to radical restructuring even when a catastrophe like a mass extinction might seem to offer the chance. 'Perhaps modern organisms could not spawn a rapid array of fundamentally new designs, no matter what the ecological opportunity.'

While this is important, it would not necessarily undermine the concept of progressive evolution. The creatures generated by the diverse body plans of the Cambrian explosion that became extinct might simply have been evolutionary experiments that failed, the 'unfit'. Life might still have led by an almost inevitable process to a form of intelligent life like us. However, it appears that the Burgess Shale species reveal 'no evidence whatsoever – not a shred – that losers in the great decimation were systematically inferior in adaptive design to those that survived'. To the question, therefore, of which body plans might have seemed most likely to succeed because of their adaptive potential, the answer appears to be that it would have been impossible to tell. The model of a simple ladder of progress or a branching tree of increasing complexity and diversity does not hold.

> The history of multicellular life has been dominated by decimation of a large initial stock, quickly generated in the Cambrian explosion. The story of the last 500 million years has featured restriction followed by proliferation within a few stereotyped designs, not general expansion of range and increase in complexity as our favoured iconography, the cone of increasing diversity, implies.

While the concept of speciation by means of natural selection holds good over long periods of time, therefore, the mass extinctions that took place after the Cambrian explosion and again during the Permian and Cretaceous periods indicate that contingency, or chance, has played a far greater part in the history of life than was previously suspected. Up to 96 per cent of marine species were lost in the Permo-Triassic extinction. As Stephen Jay Gould observes: 'When diversity plummets to 4 per cent of its former value, we must entertain the idea that some groups lose by something akin to sheer bad luck.'

What this also means is that life as it *has* evolved is 'a staggeringly improbable series of events, sensible enough in retrospect and subject to rigorous explanation, but utterly unpredictable and quite unrepeatable. Wind back the tape of life to the early days of the Burgess Shale; let it play again from an identical starting point, and the chance becomes vanishingly small that anything like human intelligence would grace the replay.'

71

Part of Stephen Jay Gould's achievement in *Wonderful Life* is his ability to give a rigorous palaeontological description of the Burgess Shale fossils which is completely open and fascinating to the non-specialist. But he is well aware of the cost to human self-esteem in the overthrow of such archetypal images as the ladder of progress and the cone of increasing diversity and of the fact that science is in a way a cruelly double-edged weapon of our understanding. For 'as Freud observed, our relationship with science must be paradoxical because we are forced to pay an almost intolerable price for each major gain in knowledge and power – the psychological cost of progressive dethronement from the centre of things, and increasing marginality in an uncaring universe.'

Scientific truth is provisional, not absolute. It is always open to revision. However, the relentless pressure of discoveries across the sciences has been to confirm this sense of marginalization and it seems unlikely that future developments will reverse it. Under these circumstances, Gould sees two possibilities:

> We may . . . accept the implications and learn to seek the meaning of human life, including the sense of morality, in other, more appropriate domains – either stoically with a sense of loss, or with joy in the challenge if our temperament be optimistic. Or we may continue to seek cosmic comfort in nature by reading life's history in a distorted light.

This statement is (uncharacteristically) not entirely clear, for he does not identify the more appropriate domains where we should or could seek the source of morality or the meaning of human life. The implication of science appears to be that we have no discernible significance, and I do not think Gould is advocating mysticism or revealed religion as a parallel way of probing reality, which might cancel out scientific understanding of the universe and return to us some kind of (undemonstrable) centrality and importance.

The only alternative would seem to be a self-defining significance, a consensus on ethics as an enclosed human value system. But it is at least open to question whether the mind can live in such a self-referential world while retaining, all the while, a sense of its own cosmic marginality. It is equally a question as to how many of us can maintain a stoic front in the light of our knowledge, and for how long. Few, I would guess, are capable of sustaining the joyous sense of challenge which Stephen Jay Gould himself so evidently has. If this is so, then Gould's second, and as he says, intellectually unacceptable alternative, is likely to remain a fixture of our thinking, for a misread nature which bestows meaning on us is a palliative many people will be unwilling to do without.

This is one of the problems with *The End of Nature*[3] by Bill McKibben which was published at the same time as *Wonderful Life*. In its way it is a wide-ranging book, for it seeks to place the significance of global warming and genetic engineering in a broader philosophical and religious context as well as to discuss their practical implications. The book in fact revolves around the questions: what is nature, and what is its meaning for humanity? But unlike Stephen Jay Gould in *Wonderful Life*, Bill McKibben does not try to reach beyond our ideological constraints to a deeper understanding of nature. Instead his thinking is governed by one such constraint, in the light of which he proceeds to interpret us and nature. The result is that his argument is flawed.

McKibben's discussion of the chemical, physical and meteorological processes involved in human induced global warming is one of the best popularizations that I have read. He draws on a wide range of scientific data and debate and is careful to tease out for the non-specialist something of the immense complexity of the problem. In his discussion of the likely effects of global warming he is equally careful to cite the range of scientific opinion, to stress the difficulty of interpreting inadequate and complex data so as to come at some idea of what is likely to happen.

All of this is excellent. Yet when McKibben turns to the meaning of nature, he abandons science and falls back rapidly to a position of entrenched nature mysticism in the tradition of Thoreau. Such a move may be valid, yet it must, it seems to me, test itself against the best of what we know about nature from other sources, especially science. The Burgess Shale tells us a great deal about nature and raises questions about our

[3] Published by Viking, 1990.

relationship to it which must at least be acknowledged and which certainly cannot be evaded by a retreat into nature mysticism. Yet this is precisely what McKibben does. He uses science when it suits him to persuade the reader of the validity of his argument, but silently abandons it when scientific examination of nature might be seen to threaten his own ideological constraint.

McKibben argues that one of our founding ideas about nature concerns its independence. No matter what inroads humanity has made upon it, nature has always seemed ultimately inviolable. But that perception is changing, for global warming *is* global and will affect all aspects of nature in the future.

> We have changed the atmosphere, and thus we are changing the weather. By changing the weather, we make every spot on earth man-made and artificial. We have deprived nature of its independence, and that is fatal to its meaning. Nature's meaning is its independence; without it there is nothing but us.

This in turn (if true) is fatal to McKibben's Romantic view of nature, and that is why it disturbs him so much. He describes himself as 'a reasonably orthodox Methodist' and a regular church-goer.

> But it is not in 'God's house' that I feel his presence most – it is in his outdoors, on some sun-warmed slope of pine needles or by the surf. It is there that the numbing categories men have devised to contain this mystery – sin and redemption and incarnation and so on – fall away, leaving the overwhelming sense of the goodness and sweetness at work in the world.

This is no more than a weak version of Charles Doolittle Walcott's 'sublime conception' of God's benevolence manifesting itself in the evolutionary process, and it is open to the same objection: it does not square up to the observable facts.

For the Romantic view of nature as a benevolent force necessary to the growth of the human spirit, and a means of approach to God, comes out of a quite specific historical context – the relationship between Western civilization and nature, established at the beginning of the Industrial Revolution and kept in some semblance of balance for the past 200 years. The experience of Wordsworth and Thoreau (and McKibben) is at least as dependent on civilization as it is on nature. Yet in their writings this dependence is masked and distorted, in order to make civilization the antagonist to the nature which is the source of our deepest religious feelings.

But Thoreau's famous year of retreat at Walden Pond was precisely that, a retreat. At any time he could have returned to civilization, as of course he knew and as in the end he did. The perceived Romantic value of nature assumes civilization as a vantage point from which to enjoy it. For Romanticism is the mind of Western civilization as it draws close to breaking humanity's age-old bondage to nature. Suddenly the wild places of the Earth become imbued with value and religious awe. They are where you go to experience the 'overwhelming sense of the goodness and sweetness at work in the world'.

Such ideas were impossible, however, before civilization was sufficiently advanced to allow us to perceive the awesomeness of nature without the fear of being engulfed by it. There is a significant example in the letters of the English poet Thomas Gray, written near the beginning of the Romantic period. In 1739 he accompanied Horace Walpole on a celebrated Grand Tour of Europe. The young men visited the Grande Chartreuse and there Gray experienced the Sublime – that sense of religious awe at the grandeur of wild nature which was to become so important a part of Romantic sensibility. Writing about it to Richard West, he declared:

> . . . I do not remember to have gone ten paces without an exclamation, that there was no restraining: not a precipice, not a torrent, not a cliff, but is pregnant with religion and poetry. There are certain scenes that would awe an atheist into belief, without the help of other argument.

But later, while he and Walpole were crossing the Alps, Gray experienced nature in another aspect which was not at all Sublime and which clearly made a deep impression on him. He prefaces his account of it in a letter to his mother by remarking that it was 'an odd accident enough', then goes on:

> Mr Walpole had a little fat black spaniel, that he was very fond of, which he sometimes used to set down, and let it run by the chaise

side. We were at that time in a very rough road, not two yards broad at most; on one side was a great wood of pines, and on the other a vast precipice; it was noon-day, and the sun shone bright, when all of a sudden, from the woodside (which was as steep upwards, as the other part was downwards) out rushed a great wolf, came close to the head of the horses, seized the dog by the throat, and rushed up the hill again with him in his mouth. This was done in less than a quarter of a minute; we all saw it, and yet the servants had not time to draw their pistols, or do anything to save the dog. If he had not been there, and the creature had thought fit to lay hold of one of the horses, chaise, and we, and all must inevitably have tumbled above fifty fathoms perpendicular down the precipice.

This account is interesting. It has the mark of real experience, something contingent, unexpected, exciting and frightening, that intrudes boldly into an ordered human world. It is notable how Gray is concerned to place the incident accurately and in simple language. There is a sense of the urgent need to *tell* which has no time for the rather stilted record of his experience of the 'Sublime' and the Grande Chartreuse.

Later in Italy Gray recovered his poise, but the event none the less haunted him, and he refers to it again in a letter to Thomas Wharton. The letter is a spoof prospectus for a book of *Travels* by 'T. G., Gent.', one chapter of which refers to the encounter with the wolf:

Sets out the latter end of November to cross the Alps. He is devoured by a wolf; and how it is to be devoured by a wolf: the seventh day he comes to the foot of Mount Cenis. How he is wrap'd up in bear-skins and beaver-skins; boots on his legs; caps on his head; muffs on his hands, and taffety over his eyes. He is placed on a bier, and is carried to heaven by the savages blindfold. How he lights among a certain nation called Clouds; how they are always in a sweat, and never speak, but they grunt; how they flock about him, and think him very odd for not doing so too. He falls plump into Italy.

This is one of the strangest pieces of writing from the mid-eighteenth century that I know. Far from coming from the hand of the author of 'Elegy Written in a Country Churchyard', it reads like the synopsis of a poem by Ted Hughes. Although the tone is meant to be light-hearted, atavistic motifs rise like bad dreams to the surface of Gray's mind. The ceremonial wrapping of his body in animal skins, the sensory deprivation of the blindfold, muffs and boots, all suggest some kind of ritual shamanistic death in which 'T. G., Gent.' passes into the power of another, non-human, confident world. This is what it is, the unconscious of Gray's mind seems to be saying, to be devoured by the wolf of nature, which holds him in an imaginative grip far more powerful than his rather empty thoughts on nature's sublimity. At the end of this fantasy, of course, he 'falls plump into Italy', the world of Classical Antiquity and the Renaissance, governed by decorum and tradition, where the poet can once more assume the role of Thomas Gray, Gentleman, and lead a civil and civilized life.

I have described Gray's experience in some detail because it goes to the centre of an ambivalence in our attitude to nature which has serious implications for the environmental crisis facing us now. The idea of the Sublime in nature is a powerful one. It has fuelled some of the greatest poetry in the English language and it is the pathway to what can be described (though very ambiguously, I think) as religious or mystical experience.

But the Romantic vision of nature was only achieved at a cost: a strange averting of the eyes from the fact that, except under very favourable circumstances, the relationship of our species with nature has been one of unending struggle. Until civilization was sufficiently advanced, nature's grandeur was a threat, and the wild places people value and seek to preserve now were avoided and feared as 'deserts'. A weakness in the early Romantic movement is its unwillingness or inability to incorporate this primal human fear into its philosophy of nature, though Coleridge in 'The Rime of the Ancyent Marinere' is a partial exception.

In this sense, the Romantics were pre-Modern, for although evolutionary ideas were beginning to circulate during their lifetime, poets like Wordsworth and Coleridge wrote before the Darwinian revolution which changed our understanding of nature, its history and our species' relation to it.

None the less, in many ways the English Romantic poets still seem remarkably modern. Reading Coleridge or Keats, it is possible to feel the presence of a contemporary sensibility, for Romanticism has survived into our times in complex ways. This is partly because it is arguably the greatest literary and philosophical movement that Western civilization has produced. But it is also because the Romantic mind is very similar to the scientific mind and it may not be going too far to say that science and Romanticism share a similar aim. For at the centre of each is the idea of the pursuit of truth as a journey which the individual has to undertake knowing that he will have to abandon much of his mental luggage on the way, that tradition may be no guide where he is going and that such journeying of the mind is lonely, unpredictable and open to intellectual and psychological shipwreck. Because of this, there has been a confluence of Romanticism and science in our century. The great Romantics of our time, Robinson Jeffers, Harry Martinson, Ted Hughes, have neither evaded the journey nor failed to confront the implications of science.

But Romanticism has also survived in a debased form as a patina on our popular culture which does evade the mind's journey by seeking false consolation in a weak version of the Sublime in nature. So Wordsworth's intimation of nature as

> the emblem of a mind
> That feeds upon infinity, that broods
> Over the dark abyss

becomes for many, in Bill McKibben's words, a 'sense of the goodness and sweetness at work in the world'.

The absurdity of this last statement ought to be evident to anyone who takes a look at the workings of nature with open eyes. At an intellectual level it is simply untenable in the light of evolutionary biology, especially the revised history of nature demanded by the evidence of the Burgess Shale fossils. Yet it survives not only in works that are in many ways perceptive, like Bill McKibben's *The End of Nature*, but as a backdrop of sentiment among certain factions in the Green movement, and in the films which almost nightly are screened on television as part of high technology's lament and farewell to a Romantically perceived nature. To understand what I mean, listen to the disjunction that often occurs between the 'voice-over', with its enumeration of zoological and environmental facts, and the yearning burden of music which accompanies the panorama of the vanishing herds of the plains, the haunted-eyed creatures of the night forest.

Bill McKibben acknowledges the shallowness of much apparent contemporary interest in nature. As he says, for many it is no more than a hobby: 'We have become in rapid order a people whose conscious need for nature is superficial.' Yet the emphasis on *conscious* need here suggests an oppositional *unconscious* need for a deeper contact with nature which remains unfulfilled. It is easy to blame this, as McKibben does, on urbanized mass society which creates a complex technological barrier between the individual and nature. I have believed this myself for many years. But now I think that the drive towards such a society over the past 200 years has itself been prompted by humanity's deepest response to nature, one so buried in our minds that we hardly know it ourselves, or recognize it in our attempts to deal consciously with nature. That response is fear, and even horror, not of course at the park-like world that most of us in the West think of as nature, nor even at the wildernesses in countries like the United States that have been set aside and are protected. The fear and horror penetrate beneath the surface of a nature we have already tamed to a perception about the very nature of life on Earth with which it is so difficult to come to terms that we try to repress it.

I have nowhere found this idea better expressed than in *The Soul of the Ape* by Eugène Marais.[4] Writing about natural selection, Marais observes that:

> There is no such thing as an organism in perfect accord with its environment. In ultimate analysis, this practical truth rests upon the certainty that all the laws of the inanimate universe are inherently hostile to organic life. The struggle of life is not, as it often appears in popular conception, merely the struggle of the organism against competing fellows. From its inception, an organism struggles against opposing laws of matter which make for dissolution and the hindrance of growth. Organic evolution is at best the line of least resistance. Selection is not so much the preservation of the fit as it is the destruction of the unfit. For the fit it is not so much a conquering invasion as a lucky escape.

And he goes on to note:

> It is no doubt a conception of this truth which colours the thread of pessimism running through all recorded human thought; the

[4] First published 1969, reprinted by Penguin in 1984.

conviction that, whatever the circumstances may be, the evil in existence must necessarily outweigh the good – as the sparks fly upward.

Though we may repress this perception from the deep psychology of our species, we can never eradicate it entirely. What the Romantic poets of the twentieth century have revealed about the dark side of nature in their art emerges also in popular culture, like magma forced from the depths under pressure. A recurring motif of science fiction films, for example, is of a high-technology future in which human beings are freed from nature. In such films, the Earth is often represented as a desert where humans live in enclosed, controlled environments and where familial and biological relationships have been replaced by ones which are formal and functional. If the setting is an alien planet, then it too is often a desert, or a place where its nature is violent, antagonistic, to be fought off and destroyed. Even in films set in our own times and in familiar surroundings, like Steven Spielberg's *Jaws*, nature is represented as something aggressive, deeply to be feared and if necessary eradicated.

This is what drives us, but at such a profound and disguised level that, when it is pointed out to us in art, our reaction to our horror is one of horror. For we did not know this consciously before and we do not like to think of life as being like this. Moreover, if we sit, as it were, looking forward, we can immerse ourselves in the future development and achievement of our high-technology civilization and forget what is driving us in the depths of the mind.

But what if the civilization we have created is destroying nature so that not only it but humanity as well must perish? This is one of the main questions in *The End of Nature*, and Bill McKibben is rightly pessimistic about the answer. As he says, 'Not only is the industrial system huge but the trend towards growth is incredibly powerful.' Moreover, as he points out, with the world's population expected to double and perhaps treble by the middle of the next century, the temptation to bank on technology to get us out of what are likely to be appalling human and environmental conditions will be immense.

McKibben sees us turning more and more to genetic engineering or 'biotechnology' as a means of staving off disaster which in turn, as he says, is likely to have unknowable and dangerous consequences as engineered organisms escape or are released into nature. For Bill McKibben, genetic engineering represents a second 'end of nature'. He suggests an alternative, based on the ideas of Dark Green movements like Earth First!, which is that we should try to develop a more humble attitude towards the Earth, seeing ourselves as one species among many – a biocentric instead of a homocentric way of looking. If in the developed nations we begin to regard ourselves in this recentred way, it could lead to a radical restructuring of our priorities and of our civilization.

It is hard to disagree. But even while he is making such a proposal there is something in Bill McKibben's tone which lets the reader know that he does not believe it is going to happen. It is not merely that we are too deeply involved in a high-technology civilization whose impetus must carry us on, almost as servants of the great industrial system we think we control. It is the fact that behind this lies the deeper fear expressed by Eugène Marais. For the truth is that most of us do not care about wild nature except as an idea of somewhere which is other than where we are. If we were placed in the middle of a real wilderness, we would be afraid. Most of us are quite content with a vision of a future Earth as a human-controlled park.

Marc Reisner makes this point in *Cadillac Desert*.[5] Writing of the artificial desert civilization that has been created this century in the vast arid zone that is the American West, he observes:

> People say that they 'love' the desert, but few of them love it enough to live there. I mean the real desert, not in a make-believe city like Phoenix, with exotic palms and golf-course lawns and a five-hundred-foot fountain and an artificial surf. Most people 'love' the desert by driving through it in air-conditioned cars, 'experiencing' its grandeur.

Bill McKibben believes that human-induced global warming has changed our relationship to nature in kind rather than degree. I think that this is debatable. Even without the green-house effect, our urge to conquer and control nature has driven

---

[5] *Cadillac Desert: The American West and its Disappearing Water* (Secker and Warburg, 1990).

us to a situation where nature in the original Romantic sense hardly exists. (Wilderness 'parks' and wildlife 'refuges' can be discounted because no matter how large they are, they are areas we have *chosen* to set aside. This alone destroys their status as nature in Bill McKibben's sense of being inviolably independent.)

This is illustrated by Marc Reisner in *Cadillac Desert*. In the process of European civilization's expansion across North America, the human species has already made an indelible mark on the nature of the continent. A quarter of a million dams have been built, the flow of rivers has been diverted and in some cases reversed; the great Ogallala Aquifer that extends from South Dakota to west Texas, and which has stored vast quantities of water from several ice ages, has been depleted in a couple of generations of ruthless and ultimately unsustainable irrigation farming. The impact on American natural life has been devastating:

> Glen Canyon is gone. The Colorado Delta is dead. The Missouri bottomlands have disappeared. Nine out of ten acres of wetlands in California have vanished, and with them millions of migratory birds. The great salmon runs in the Columbia, the Sacramento, the San Joaquin, and dozens of tributaries are diminished or extinct. The prairie is civilized and dull; its last wild features, the pothole marshes in the Dakotas, could all but disappear at the hands of the Garrison Dam and Cendak projects if they are ever built.

Bill McKibben is aware of this, of course: it is what he is trying to stop. But the merit of *Cadillac Desert* is that Marc Reisner shows in detail how a federal and state legislature meshed with government agencies and vested engineering and economic interests, has created a structure so powerful that it seems as if it cannot be diverted, but must grind on even if it leads (as Reisner believes) to a ruined civilization claimed again by the desert sands.

Like Bill McKibben, I find the Dark Green alternative attractive, but in such an overcrowded world there is unlikely to be any escape from the technological imperative we have created. McKibben himself is almost a paradigm of the dilemma. He lives, he tells us, in a log house in the Adirondack Mountains. He has a car but bikes as much as he can. But as he sits by his wood fire in the quiet of the hills, he can also send or receive messages on his fax machine. He acquired it, he says, 'on the premise that it makes for graceful, environmentally sound communication'. It seems to me that that premiss is false. The fax machine predicates the vast complexity of the very high-technology civilization that McKibben is against. It is possible for the individual to choose an 'environmentally sound' piece of high-tech machinery, but its existence assumes a myriad other high-technology options which are not separable because they are locked in a self-sustaining and self-perpetuating system. Like most of us, Bill McKibben would like to have it both ways. But it is not possible.

What will happen in the next fifty to a hundred years is dark and uncertain. *Dirigiste* government on a global scale may be able to reduce the human population against predictions, while technology, especially genetic engineering, may solve many of the problems which at present seem insuperable. On the other hand, over-population and global pollution may be leading us towards some form of ecological collapse and with it the prospect of mass extinction. In *Wonderful Life*, Stephen Jay Gould writes that mass extinctions have been *'more frequent, rapid, devastating in magnitude* and *distinctly different in effect* than we formerly imagined. Mass extinctions, in other words, seem to be genuine disruptions in geological flow, not merely the high points of a continuity' (Gould's emphasis).

Because of the geological time-scale involved, the mass extinctions of the past seem immensely distant from us, almost as if they were a phase in the history of the Earth that is long past. It is difficult psychologically to consider that there is no reason why mass extinctions should not continue to occur, and that we may have triggered forces which will lead to one that could engulf our own species. As Stephen Jay Gould notes, we like to think of this as the Age of the Mammals, and among them ourselves, the Earth's most successful species. Extinction is for the dinosaurs – creatures that could not cope. But this is a homocentric way of looking at things. There is a stronger case for considering it the Age of the Arthropods, since, according to Gould, 'some 80 per cent of all named animal species are arthropods, the vast majority insects'.

Like many others writing about the environment, Bill McKibben deals with too short a time-span, and is open to the charge of homocentricity which, at the end of the book, he urges us to abandon. It is interesting that there is no entry in his index for 'extinction' or 'mass extinction', though it has to be seriously considered whether this is what we are faced with as a species.

If such a (for us) cataclysmic event occurs, extinction will also be the fate of many other species. Species could plummet to the near-disastrous survival rate of 4 per cent as happened for marine species at the juncture of the Permian and Triassic periods. It would be the end of our kind of intelligent life and it would be the end of a period of the natural history of the Earth, which Bill McKibben identifies as 'nature'.

But it would not necessarily be the end of life on Earth. The sun, after all, is only half-way through its life-cycle. There are several thousand million years for surviving species to diversify (and among them, likely as not, members of the phylum Arthropoda). Nature in this deep sense would continue – a fact which I find consoling, though I am not sure that I could say why.

Postscript

The Burgess Shale fossils are the subject of intense debate among palaeontologists, and Stephen Jay Gould's interpretation has not gone unchallenged.[6] In particular it is argued that there are far fewer unique phyla among the fossils than Gould claims. Since the publication of *Wonderful Life* in 1990, several key species that Gould allotted to phyla of their own have been reclassified into groups with modern descendants. Gould's emphasis on the role of chance in the creation of the Cambrian 'explosion' and the sudden extinctions that followed it has also been questioned. Some palaeontologists argue that the Cambrian can be accounted for in normal evolutionary terms without invoking chance.

Gould counters that the reclassification of some key species does not invalidate his overall argument. The identification and classification of such ancient fossils is immensely difficult. It may be some time before a consensus is reached, based on further

[6] See Tim Beardsley, 'Weird wonders', *Scientific American* (June 1992); Henry Gee, 'Something completely different', *Nature* (6 August 1992); Jeffrey S. Levington, 'The Big Bang of animal evolution', *Scientific American* (November 1992). Also Gould, 'Defending the heretical and the superfluous' and 'The development of *Hallucigenia*', in *Eight Little Piggies* (Penguin, 1994).

analysis of the Burgess Shale fossils and related fossils from other more recently discovered sites. Whether or not Gould's hypothesis has to be radically revised or even abandoned, the Cambrian was clearly a period of rapid change at a crucial period in the development of multicellular life with hard tissues.

7

Poetry and the new nature

In 'Resolution and Independence', Wordsworth presents us with an enigma: an old man motionless by a moorland pool. His leech-gatherer is so familiar from literary tradition that it is easy to forget how strange he is, or rather, how strange Wordsworth's representation of him is – almost as if the old man belongs to a different species and Wordsworth is seeing him for the first time. In an attempt to describe what is before him, the poet grasps at analogies. The leech-gatherer is like a huge stone, a sea-beast, a cloud – images which combine a sense of immense age, weight, cumbrous movement, stillness and evanescence; contraries that are held without contradiction in a single being

> . . . not all alive nor dead,
> Nor all asleep – in his extreme old age.

This is a being who takes many shapes in Wordsworth's poems: Michael, the old Cumberland beggar, the shepherds in *The Prelude*, the mother in 'The Thorn', the forsaken Indian woman, figures which leave a composite impression on the mind. Through them, Wordsworth revises in ways which are still startling our sense of relationship to nature, making us contemplate ourselves as isolated objects in a landscape.

There is more in the poems, of course, including the moral lessons which Wordsworth consciously skimmed from the experiences they convey. But the troubling image of the leech-gatherer whose voice is 'like a stream' sets up reverberations which are distinctly modern. 'The proper study of Mankind is Man,' wrote Pope, who thought he knew what mankind was. Between his time and ours, however, there is the leech-gatherer with his strangeness, raising the question not 'who am I?' but 'what am I?' In modern times we have had to begin the study of our kind again.

The pivot of that study is Charles Darwin's *The Origin of Species*, published nine years after Wordsworth's death. The evolution of species by means of natural selection depends on the hypothesis that the Earth is immensely old and predicates that human beings are members of an evolved species, *Homo sapiens*, different from other living forms, though related to them. In the past 130 years, research in geology, palaeontology, zoology, biochemistry, anthropology and a dozen related disciplines has confirmed the general truth of Darwin's theory. The knowledge has transformed us, because we have learnt that we are not at the mid-point between animals and angels, and that the Earth is not a staging post on the way to a better life. It is 'neither a bad variant nor a tryout', as Ted Hughes expressed it in 'Pibroch'. In the post-Darwinian world it is as if we stood up and looked about us for the first time.

What we see is glorious, but also frightening. The ability to objectify ourselves as a living form, a phenomenon in nature, is an immense intellectual achievement. Yet at the same time it diminishes us. In Ted Hughes's poem 'The Howling of Wolves', the wolf shivers in the northern forest:

> The earth is under its tongue,
> A dead weight of darkness, trying to see through its eyes.
> The wolf is living for the earth.
> But the wolf is small, it comprehends little.

The metaphor is a powerful one: the Earth using its creatures as a means to see, minimally in the case of the wolf, but more comprehensively through *Homo sapiens*.

The mind that can think of life 'seeing' for the Earth, however, must also think of itself in complex ways. Consciousness produces a sense of self which we like to think of as unique; we feel to a degree separate from nature because of our ability to articulate what we are. For centuries we have felt different from the animals, distinguished by our possession of a soul.

Many in the West still believe in the soul (or half-believe in it), because it bestows a sense of dignity and offers the hope that something of us will survive death. But the idea of the soul depends on the conviction, familiar to us from Genesis, that the Earth was created by a single act of God, so that its creatures sprang complete onto the plains and into the forests, including humanity with its divine spark. However, geology, palae-ontology and evolutionary theory have destroyed the material basis for such a belief. If *Homo sapiens* has a soul, did *Homo neanderthalensis* and *Homo erectus* and *Homo habilis*? And should we include earlier hominidae such as *Australopithecus africanus* and *Australopithecus afarensis*? If so, what about the super-family of the hominoidea which includes the great apes and to which we belong? No wonder the Church reacted negatively to the publication of *The Origin of Species*, or that in America funda-mentalists invented a pseudo-science, creationism, to explain evolutionary theory away.

But then, who bothers to ask questions about the soul, except Christians? To the majority it is like debating the number of angels on a pinhead, irrelevant to the pursuit of happiness in life. Our fear of death, however, is as intense as before. In 'The Howling of Wolves', the wolf's eyes

> never learn how it has come about
> That they must live like this . . .

The wolf's limited consciousness is its agony. Our problem is that we see too clearly, aware of ourselves as separate entities yet knowing that we cannot escape nature's processes and that what brought us into consciousness will also destroy us. When pressed to the edge, nature, the self and death become objects of terror to the modern mind.

This is what happens to the rather cowardly figure of Willems in Joseph Conrad's *An Outcast of the Islands*. He has been abandoned and left to die, as he thinks, in a riverbank clearing in the rain forest. He is overwhelmed, at the thought of his death, by a degrading fear which is the product of the mind's consciousness. Because of it, Willems can think of himself as an object, yet at the same time he feels intensely about his condition in a personal way. The sense of separation from his environment and the ability to imagine the thriving life all around him, which will continue after he is dead, make his mind a kind of hell:

> . . . All this would remain – remain for years, for ages, for ever. After he had miserably died here, all this would remain, would live, would exist in joyous sunlight, would breathe in the coolness of serene nights. What for, then? He would be dead. He would be stretched upon the warm moisture of the ground, feeling nothing, seeing nothing, knowing nothing; he would lie stiff, passive, rotting slowly; while over him, under him, through him – unopposed, busy, hurried – the endless and minute throngs of insects, little shining monsters of repulsive shapes, with horns, with claws, with pincers, would swarm in streams, in rushes, in eager struggle for his body; would swarm countless, persistent, ferocious and greedy – till there would remain nothing but the white gleam of bleaching bones in the long grass that would shoot its feathery heads between the bare and polished ribs. There would be that only left of him; nobody would miss him; no one would remember him.

Ideas take time to percolate down, even in the modern age, and it is only in our century, I think, that Willems's fear has been kindled in the majority – a feeling, rather than a train of thought, as to the implications of evolutionary theory for human nature. The sum of our knowledge expands, but, in inverse proportion, there is a general sense of the lessening of individual possibility, a material, biochemical diminution of what we once thought humanity to be like.

In the West, society consoles itself with the tatters of liberal-humanism. We act as if our lives had dignity and meaning, but the 'as if' threatens to overwhelm us with something close to despair. It can be repressed but it will not go away, eddying to the surface in swirls of mass hysteria and violence and in the neuroses of individuals that are a cry for help. The dominant emotions of the age are anxiety and anger.

Robinson Jeffers perceived this of American society in the 1920s and 1930s. In 'The Purse-Seine' he describes how Pacific Coast fishermen located sardines at night by their phosphor-escence, casting their nets and hauling the fish tighter and tighter until panic and fear whipped the water 'to a pool of flame'. He uses it as a metaphor for life in the modern cities. Looking down on one at night from a mountain, the extended glitter of lights reminds him of the fish. Caught in the mass urbanized life of the times, we are in a purse-seine of our own making:

> . . . We have geared the machines and locked all
> together into interdependence; we have built the great
> cities; now
> There is no escape. We have gathered vast populations incapable
> of free survival, insulated
> From the strong earth, each person in himself helpless, on all
> dependent. The circle is closed, and the net
> Is being hauled in. They hardly feel the chords drawing, yet
> they shine already.

Robinson Jeffers's most memorable poems are about men and women who destroy themselves, and each other, fuelling passions that cannot be satisfied because they make demands on life that are unrealistic. He puts much of the blame for this on Christianity, whose notion of a God of Love breaks again and again on the reality of our experience of the Earth. For Jeffers, God is immanent in all aspects of the post-Darwinian, post-Einsteinian universe, and human beings are peripheral rather than, as Christianity would have it, central. Jeffers believed that recognition of our marginality freed us from the desire and self-concern on which Western civilization is built. The individual should cultivate a stoic indifference to humanity which he called, aggressively, Inhumanism: 'Turn outward from each other, so far as need and kindness permit, to the vast life and inexhaustible beauty beyond humanity.'

Ted Hughes is the direct inheritor of Jeffers. In *Lupercal* and *Wodwo*, he re-creates the intense being of other creatures, with sensibilities very different from our own. In poems like 'Thrushes' and 'Skylarks', he comes as close as possible to wrenching us from our habitual human-centred way of looking. Those who dismiss them as 'animal' poems fail to see what he is doing. In daily life, what we see is largely prefabricated by what we expect to see. Ted Hughes reacts to the skylark as Wordsworth did to the leech-gatherer – he sees as if for the first time, seizing every kind of analogy to describe the strangeness of what is before him.

Crow goes on to explore humanity in a similar way. Wordsworth, at the further edge of modern times, could still find consolation in the old man in the tract of lonely moor. But the post-Darwinian world forces us to look again. *Crow* is a great stripping away of Western civilization under the pressure of the scientific imperative: look closely at the object; describe what you see. Crow is born as if dropped onto Earth, with no civilization to give him ethical preconceptions but with a powerful primitive intelligence. Under these conditions, he starts from scratch.

Crow is Romantic in the Coleridgean sense that it assumes that the mind interferes with what it sees: we perceive rather than see. It is also Wordsworthian in that it recognizes that our deepest assumptions about life are founded on nature. However, Crow is born into a post-Romantic, Darwinian world, from which he draws different inferences from those of Wordsworth:

Crow saw the herded mountains, steaming in the morning.
And he saw the sea
Dark-spined, with the whole earth in its coils.
He saw the stars, fuming away into the black, mushrooms of the
    nothing forest, clouding their spores, the virus of God.

And he shivered with the horror of Creation.

One of the most memorable photographs of the century shows the Earth as seen from space. At last the Earth sees itself entire, through our eyes. The human mind, however, is relentless; it cannot stop but must go on. In 1989 *Voyager 2* extended our sight with photographs of Neptune, the massive aqua-blue planet, white clouds rippling for hundreds of miles across its opaque atmosphere. *Voyager's* last picture, taken as it sped out of the solar system for ever, showed the southern edge of Neptune and the crescent of its moon, Triton, shining in the pale light of the distant sun. June Kinoshita described the planet in *Scientific American* as a 'looming belly', and that is exactly what it looks like, cold and pregnant with implication.

Wordsworth was an old man when Neptune was discovered 150 years ago. Where does the environment begin and end? The eye expands like a glistening, inquisitive ball, in all directions.

We are amazed by what we see, yet it also makes us afraid, for we do not wish to be born into the world which our knowledge insists is there.

Robinson Jeffers and Ted Hughes expose the fierce contradictions in this: they are poets of the new nature. But although they ask the right questions, their answers are less satisfactory. Jeffers himself recognized that stoicism is too unaccommodating for the majority of people. It is almost impossible to avoid breaking down into feeling, and involvement in the world. After *Crow*, on the other hand, Ted Hughes falls back on a nature mysticism which seems to me at odds with our knowledge. Poems like *Gaudete* try to impose a belief on us, with a contingent symbolism, which we can no longer believe in simply as the *truth* – though we may regret its loss, and look longingly to other societies more 'primitive' than our own, where such a belief still seems possible.

In the end, neither Robinson Jeffers nor Ted Hughes is what might be termed a healing poet, as Wordsworth was. But perhaps this is impossible in our times. There is a growing air of defeat about us which all the business of politics and economics, the momentous events in Eastern Europe, Russia and the European Community, can hardly disguise. It is not just that we are poisoning the environment or may destroy ourselves in a nuclear war, but that we do not know what to do with our minds. No poet, it may be, can tell us that.

8

A look at Gaia

It is rare for a scientist to become a guru, in the sixties' sense of the word. Yet this is what has happened to James Lovelock, proponent of the Gaia hypothesis that the Earth is a single living organism. At the same time, in inverse proportion to 'Gaia's' popularity among Greens, scientists in the various disciplines affected have received it with scepticism, and members of the scientific community who have supported Lovelock, such as Lyn Margulis in the United States, have done so at the risk of their own professional reputations. It may be, as opponents contend, that the hypothesis is wrong, or it may be that it challenges too many entrenched positions within current orthodoxy to gain even grudging acceptance. Either way, many, including James Lovelock, would agree that more research is needed to test the most fundamental propositions of the.Gaia hypothesis before it can be easily dismissed or fully accepted.

'Images' have a powerful role in our society, so much so that one which is perceived as negative can easily stifle an individual's curiosity. I was put off by what I conceived to be James Lovelock's ideas, partly by such things as the 'Gaia' posters (with that famous picture of Earth taken from space) which seem to adorn the walls of every wholefood shop in Britain. For though I use wholefood shops, their aura of health and goodness makes me ill at ease. I buy what I want and then quietly slip away.

However, a recent article in *Scientific American* gave me an overview of the current state of the Gaia controversy in scientific circles which made the hypothesis sound interesting. So, setting aside my distaste for the posters and my feeling that wholefood-shop goodness is next to a certain kind of irritating smugness, I decided to go away and read James Lovelock's books, *Gaia* and *The Ages of Gaia*.[1]

What I found was not what I had expected. In the first place, James Lovelock is not only an independent scientist (that is, unaffiliated to any university, industry or other organization), he is also an independent thinker whose ideas cannot easily be categorized and thus embraced or dismissed. Although his name is associated with the environmental movement, for example, some of his thinking sets him distinctly apart from any main-stream Green orthodoxy.

Take nuclear energy. James Lovelock is far from being a supporter of or an apologist for the nuclear industry, but in *The Ages of Gaia* he is highly critical of what he sees as the near hysteria of public attitudes to nuclear energy. He concedes that people's fear is understandable, but he does not think that it is necessarily justified. Rather it is symptomatic of something else: the fact that most of us this century live our lives at a great remove from science. 'Fear feeds on ignorance, and a great niche was opened for fear when science became incomprehensible to those who were not its practitioners.'

A great niche was also opened, he argues, for the practitioners themselves. Nuclear energy, he reminds us, was not invented by humans; it is common to the universe and was essential to the creation of Earth. Low-level radiation from nuclear processes is found naturally everywhere in the environment. But research, for example, into the relationship between nuclear emissions and disease, the results of which are always hyped by the media, feeds into our fear, because we do not possess the basic science necessary to understand, let alone evaluate, the evidence. So researchers, in turn, might be seen to have a vested interest in our ignorance: 'Consider the size and intricacy of the radiation-monitoring agencies, of the industry that builds monitoring and protective devices, and of the academic community that has radiation biology as its subject. If the strong public fear of

[1] *Gaia* (Oxford University Press, 1979; reprinted 1989); *The Ages of Gaia* (Oxford University Press, 1988; reprinted 1990).

radiation were dispelled, it would not be helpful to their continued employment.'

James Lovelock realizes that such thoughts are not popular in Green circles. 'To my ecologist friends, many of whom have been at the sharp end of the protest against nuclear power, these views must seem like a betrayal.' But he writes as a scientist, and as a scientist, '. . . I have never regarded nuclear radiation or nuclear power as anything other than a normal and inevitable part of the environment. Our prokaryotic forebears evolved on a planet-sized lump of fallout from a star-sized nuclear explosion, a supernova that synthesized the elements that go to make our planet and ourselves.' James Lovelock argues here neither for nor against nuclear power as a source of energy for humans, but against our basic ignorance of the nature of nuclear power and radiation. The hype surrounding the nuclear energy debate is what disturbs him, because it 'diverts us from the real and serious problem of living in harmony with ourselves and the rest of the biota'.

Yet it is a reaction to what might be termed 'the weak theory' of environmentalism (the living-in-harmony-with-ourselves-and-the-biota), embraced by a certain kind of pop-Green as a half-hearted and sentimental compromise, which helped put me off the Gaia hypothesis in the first place, because the two had become associated in my mind.

Turning to the books, *Gaia* and *The Ages of Gaia,* a different picture emerges. For a start, James Lovelock is a severe critic of what he calls 'the recent heresies of humanism and Marxism': he attacks, for instance, the 'feeble humanist grounds' for saving the tropical rain forests because they may 'carry plants with drugs that could cure human disease'. Referring to a vicious smog he experienced on a summer day on Dartmoor in 1982, the result of exhaust pollution brought on the airflow from Europe, he comments:

This vision of a blighted summer's day somehow encapsulates the conflict between the flabby good intentions of the humanist dream and the awful consequences of its near realisation. Let every family be free to drive into the countryside so that they can enjoy its fresh air and scenic beauty; but when they do, it all fades away in the foul haze that their collective motorized presence engenders.

Anyone who thinks 'I've done my bit for the environment', as a recent television advert put it, by turning to Ecover products, insulating the roof and perhaps fitting a catalytic converter to the car, will find little consolation in the ideas of James Lovelock:

> Gaia theory is out of tune with the broader humanist world as it is with established science. In Gaia we are just another species, neither the owners nor the stewards of this planet. Our future depends much more upon a right relationship with Gaia than with the never-ending drama of human interest.

'It is', he reminds us, 'the health of the planet that matters, not that of some individual species of organisms.' Humans, in 'Gaian' terms, are expendable, and if we upset the balance of nature too much, Gaia will eradicate us, while nature – which is far more robust than we think, according to Lovelock – will continue to evolve in a myriad different ways. He adds a rider to the effect that 'I am not mocking those environmental scientists whose life work is concern with these threats to human life'. It is merely that 'I wish only to speak out for Gaia because there are so few who do, when compared to the multitudes who speak for people'. None the less, this aspect of James Lovelock's thinking aligns him with Dark Green movements like Earth First! and has antecedents in the 'Inhumanist' ideas of the American poet Robinson Jeffers (though neither is referred to in the books).

Yet as I suggested, he is a difficult man to categorize and he is no Dark Green in any simple sense either. 'Could it be', he speculates in *Gaia*, 'that pollution is natural? If by pollution we mean the dumping of waste matter there is indeed ample evidence that pollution is as natural to Gaia as is breathing to ourselves and other animals.' He argues that the pollution caused by the Industrial Revolution is a 'relatively minor environmental upheaval' compared with the catastrophe 1.5 billion years ago when free oxygen appeared in the atmosphere and was all but fatal to the anaerobic organisms (organisms that live without free oxygen) which dominated the Earth at the time and for which oxygen was a deadly poison. It took millions of years 'until a new ecosystem made up of those resistant to oxygen inherited the surface of the Earth'. 'The very concept of pollution', he suggests, 'is anthropocentric and it may even be irrelevant in the Gaian context.'

James Lovelock is not, here, diminishing the seriousness of pollution due to human activity, which has already changed 'major chemical cycles of the planet'. It is merely that as a scientist he insists on seeing pollution in the context of geophysiology[2] with its vast time-scale as a backdrop to our human-centred concerns. Like nuclear radiation, pollution and its control have to be understood in the broad context of the Earth's history, rather than blindly feared.

If, that is, human pollution *can* be controlled, given the exponential growth of the world's population and its expected consequences. Here again James Lovelock's approach is interesting and stimulating. A lifetime's study in the Earth sciences tends to make an individual sanguine about the life expectancy of a species and the prospect of extinction. Borrowing the concept of punctuated equilibrium, first proposed by Stephen Jay Gould and Niles Eldredge as a modification to evolutionary theory, Lovelock argues that 'Gaia's' history has been one of long periods of stability followed by catastrophic change, as happened when free oxygen appeared in the atmosphere. 'We are ourselves the product of one such catastrophe. Could it be', he speculates, 'that we are unwittingly precipitating another punctuation that will alter the environment to suit our successors?'

James Lovelock does not think that the game is up for humanity, but he does insist that the immensity and complexity of the problems facing us as a species should be met head on. And the greatest of these is the exponential increase in the Earth's human population. He writes:

No one knows what is the optimum number for the human species. The analytic equipment needed to provide the answer is not yet assembled. Assuming the present per capita use of energy, we can guess that at less than 10,000 million we should still be in a Gaian world [i.e. one in which the complex forces of life operate as a self-regulating system]. But somewhere beyond this figure, especially if the consumption of energy increases, lies the final choice of permanent enslavement on the prison hulk Earth, or gigadeath to enable the survivors to restore a Gaian world.

[2] Lovelock's term for 'Gaia science'.

If there is a chance, Lovelock believes that it will be through technological advance, especially in the form of sustainable technology, and through the development of scientific 'futurology'. And here again his thinking parts company with certain factions of the Green movement. For, he insists, 'there can be no voluntary resignation from technology. We are so inextricably part of the technosphere that giving it up is as unrealistic as jumping off a ship in mid-Atlantic to swim the rest of the journey in glorious independence.'

But such realization brings in its trail further problems. The 'technosphere' – at least for the present – is intimately connected with the development of cities, the mass urban environment where most of us live and which, Lovelock argues, acts as a kind of sensory deprivation, deadening our response to the larger world of 'Gaia'. For 'city life reinforces and strengthens the heresy of humanism, that narcissistic devotion to human interests alone.'

And this raises another doubt in Lovelock's train of thought. If he is right that we must depend on a scientific-technological futurology to help anticipate imbalances in the 'Gaian' system (due to human activity) which in turn will enable us to take preventive action, then we must depend on the scientists and the predictive models they devise. Here is the problem. For like the rest of us, scientists are largely city-dwellers; the city is where they live and work and few of them have much direct contact with nature. As a result, he claims, they suffer from the same kind of sensory deprivation as the rest of the population. Because of this, Lovelock fears that many scientists are out of touch with the living world and that the predictive models they create, from immense amounts of data, are in fact false models, so that dependence on them may lead to the wrong preventive action.

But what of the model implicit in James Lovelock's hypothesis? It can be argued that it is at once boldly simple and extremely complex. In his first book, Lovelock defined 'Gaia' as 'a complex entity involving the Earth's biosphere, atmosphere, oceans, and soil; the totality constituting a feedback or cybernetic system which seeks an optimal physical and chemical environment for life on this planet. The maintenance of relatively constant conditions by active control may be conveniently described by the term "homeostasis".'

James Lovelock was led to this conclusion through his research into pollution of the atmosphere when it occurred to him that the nature and extent of the *disequilibrium* in the chemistry of the Earth's atmosphere (as opposed to the chemical equilibrium of the atmosphere of lifeless planets such as Venus and Mars) must be

> not merely a biological product, but more probably a biological construction: not living, but like a cat's fur, a bird's feathers, or the paper of a wasp's nest, an extension of a living system designed to maintain a chosen environment. Thus the atmospheric concentration of gases such as oxygen and ammonia is found to be kept at an optimum value from which even small departures could have disastrous consequences for life.

It may seem only a small step from viewing the Earth as a cybernetic system, that is, a self-regulating system of controls and communications, necessary for the maintenance of the optimum conditions for life, to the view that the Earth itself is alive. This is 'Gaia', named after the ancient Greek Earth goddess (on the suggestion of William Golding), and used by Lovelock to identify what is in fact a huge conceptual leap to the hypothesis that all life on Earth constitutes 'a single living entity, capable of manipulating the Earth's atmosphere to suit its overall needs and endowed with faculties and powers far beyond those of its constituent parts'.

These words are from *Gaia*. A decade on, in the introduction to *The Ages of Gaia*, James Lovelock admits that 'the idea that the Earth is alive is at the outer bounds of scientific credibility', but sets out determinedly to prove that nevertheless it is so. It is over this issue that the scientific controversy rages and it is at this point that the non-specialist begins to feel out of his or her depth. For while the hypothesis itself is relatively easy to grasp, the evidence for and against, marshalled from a dozen scientific disciplines, is not. Inevitably the lay person is forced to retreat to a position of interested observer, uncertain in his or her evaluation of the validity of evidence, or of inferences drawn from it, when the scientists themselves are in such open disagreement.

In the years since the publication of *Gaia*, Lovelock has made some headway. As he says in *The Ages of Gaia*, 'most Earth scientists today accept that the reactive gases of the atmosphere are biological products'. But the most persistent criticism of the hypothesis has been that it is teleological – that it is guilty of the scientific heresy of viewing developments as being due to the purpose or design that is apparently served by them. In other words, the 'Gaia' hypothesis puts the cart before the horse. Scientists might now agree that the biota (the mass of living organisms) are the source of the atmosphere's reactive gases, and that the concentration of these gases is remarkably stable over long periods of time, but as James Lovelock admits in *The Ages of Gaia*, 'most would disagree that the biota in any way control the composition of the atmosphere, or any of the important variables, such as global temperature and oxygen concentration, which depend on the atmosphere'.

To refute the charge that the Gaia hypothesis is teleological, he devised a conceptual model which he called Daisyworld – an Earth-sized planet covered with daisies ranging from dark to neutral to light in colour. This simple flora, Lovelock argues, could easily constitute a simple cybernetic system controlling the planet's temperature by changes in the relative proportions of dark to light daisies. If the temperature drops, dark daisies which have a greater ability to absorb sunlight, and so heat, will be favoured; if the temperature rises, white daisies will spread at the expense of dark ones, because their ability to reflect sunlight will enable them to keep cool. Such a simple regulatory system requires no 'foresight or planning'. 'This is', Lovelock claims in *The Ages of Gaia*, 'a definitive rebuttal of the accusation that the Gaia hypothesis is teleological, and so far it remains unchallenged.'

However, there is another objection to the Gaia hypothesis which James Lovelock admits is harder to refute: 'that biological regulation is only partial, and that the real world is a "coevolution" of life and the inorganic'. His second book, *The Ages of Gaia*, is, in part, an attempt to answer this objection, though it is an open question as to how far he succeeds, for at several crucial points he pushes the available evidence too far (or so it seems to me as a layman) in his own favoured direction.

An example is his discussion of ocean salinity. Lovelock points out that most organisms can only tolerate salt at concentrations below 6 per cent by weight. 'Have the oceans always kept below this critical limit of salinity by chance?' he asks. 'Or has the tightly coupled evolution of life and the environment led to the automatic regulation of ocean salinity?' In other words, is control of ocean salinity the result of Gaian cybernetics?

Most salt is evaporated out of the oceans in lagoons that exist along the edges of continents. Many of these in turn become covered by sediments and are stored in the Earth's crust only to be released again into the seas as they become exposed as a result of crustal erosion. Nevertheless, as Lovelock remarks, new evaporite lagoons are constantly being formed, so that 'the balance of erosion and formation seems always to have kept enough salt sequestered in evaporite beds to keep the oceans fresh and fit for life'. The question is whether this is a purely geophysical phenomenon, a lucky chance, which keeps salinity below the crucial 6-per-cent limit that favours life, or is it an example of a 'Gaian' negative feedback, part, as James Lovelock puts it, 'of the tightly coupled evolution of life and the rocks'?

Evaporite lagoons exist behind limestone reefs that act as boundaries on the seaward side, and reefs are of course the product of living organisms. There are good reasons why reefs occur where they do, because the shallow water at the margins of continents are 'where the abundance of both nutrients and calcium bicarbonate are highest' and both are necessary to the micro-organisms which build the reefs. There is, then, a relationship between the reef-building micro-organisms, the creation of evaporite lagoons and ocean salinity. Despite the evidence which James Lovelock musters, however, it is hard to see this as anything more than a fortuitous interplay of geophysical and organic processes, which has lucky consequences for oceanic life. But Lovelock pushes his argument even further:

> At first the reef building would have only a local effect, but over time the sheer mass of the limestone would begin to affect the plastic crust of the Earth's surface, depressing it and so extending the size of the lagoon. New rock formers would always be colonizing the surface of the reef as it descended, so tending to keep the lagoon intact. If, as Don Anderson has suggested, the motion of the Earth's crust depends on the continuous deposition of calcium carbonate in the sea, the limestone reefs could have led to the complex events of mountain

building and the folding of rocks at the continental margins. This, in turn, would extend the range of shorelines where evaporite lagoons could form.

And so even plate tectonics and mountain building are drawn into an overarching negative feedback loop controlled by 'Gaia' in pursuit of the optimum conditions for life. But this statement contains a number of big 'ifs'. James Lovelock notes that 'the steps, from the individual lowering of calcium ions within the cells of a living organism to the movement of the plates, are all those that tend to improve the environment for the organisms responsible'. However, he is constrained to add that 'the links between biomineralization, salt stress, and plate tectonics are so tenuous that most scientists would think them to be connected by chance rather than geophysiology'.

While there is much to be said for his idea that the *biota* are involved in a cybernetic system which is carefully balanced, and with which humanity interferes at its own peril, the hypothesis that the Earth itself is a single living organism seems to me strained, a concept which is interesting but which is not, at least for the moment, supported by sufficient evidence. Belief in 'Gaia' still requires a leap of faith.

Yet outside the scientific community it seems that there are many people who are willing to make that leap – though in a religious rather than a scientific spirit. James Lovelock's account of the popular response to *Gaia* is interesting:

> When I wrote the first book on Gaia I had no inkling that it would be taken as a religious book. Although I thought the subject was mainly science, there was no doubt that many readers found otherwise. Two-thirds of the letters received, and still coming in, are about the meaning of Gaia in the context of religious faith . . . I was naive to think that a book about Gaia could be taken as science only.

After reading the two books, it is hard not to feel that James Lovelock was being more than a little naïve, for the choice of the name of the Greek Earth goddess for his hypothesis freighted it from the start with anthropomorphic associations which are unfortunate. It is true that in the preface of *Gaia* he warns the reader that his use of the word 'Gaia' and his reference to 'her' and 'she' are only a convenience, a shorthand for the hypothesis itself which should in no way be taken to mean that he believes 'Gaia' to be sentient. But this fails completely to take into account the subliminal effect of such language on the reader and the way in which its persistent use pushes his argument towards the anthropomorphism and indeed teleology which he wishes to avoid. He writes, for example, of 'Gaia's intelligence network', and wonders 'What parts of herself . . . does she use as a thermostat?' and so on, constantly referring to 'her' and 'she'.

Despite James Lovelock's disclaimer in the preface to *Gaia*, this kind of language has inherent implications of sentience and intent, purposefulness and consciousness. Lovelock clearly did not *mean* any of this to be taken literally, but the point is that without a continuous and conscious effort to depersonify such language on the part of the reader, it inevitably affects the emotional tone of Lovelock's argument, humanizing it in ways which make it easy for the uncritical, non-scientific mind searching for 'meaning' to latch onto 'Gaia' not as a scientific hypothesis, but as a quasi-religious phenomenon. Had he called his first book 'Toward a Cybernetic Theory of the Earth' and referred to his hypothesis as 'it' instead of naming it after the anthropomorphic Gaia, the book would never have reached so wide an audience, but nor would the hypothesis have been wrenched away from its basis in scientific speculation to fulfil what seems to me an understandable but dubious need for human meaning.

This response caused James Lovelock to write a chapter on 'God and Gaia' in his second book, *The Ages of Gaia*, which reveals, to my mind, a disappointing interference from the popular, vaguely religious notion of 'Gaia' with Lovelock's generally more stringent mode of thinking. He speculates, for instance, about the Virgin Mary who is the centre of so much Catholic devotion because, he suggests, she is more approachable than a remote, all-powerful God. 'Mary is close and can be talked to. She is believable and manageable.' However, what if there is more to her than this?

What if Mary is another name for Gaia? Then her capacity for virgin birth is no miracle or parthenogenic aberration, it is a role of Gaia since life began. Immortals do not need to reproduce an image of themselves; it is enough to renew continuously the life that constitutes them. Any living organism a quarter as old as the Universe itself and still full of vigour is as near immortal as we ever need to know. She is of the Universe and, conceivably, a part of God. On Earth she is the source of life everlasting and is alive now; she gave birth to humankind and we are a part of her.

This is to anthropomorphize the Earth with a vengeance. Among many things, it begs the question of why a cybernetic system should be identified with the female principle in the first place, as well as how and why it should be venerated in religious terms. Moreover, equating the Virgin Mary with Gaia reflects only the more benign aspects of life on Earth – if we are to anthropomorphize at all, a more suitable deity would be the Hindu goddess Kali, as James Lovelock admits a few pages later, quoting Aldous Huxley's description of her as 'at once the infinitely kind and loving mother and the terrifying Goddess of destruction, who has a necklace of skulls and drinks the blood of human beings from a skull'.

But all this is in any case to deal in metaphor and a symbology in which James Lovelock clearly does not 'believe'. As he says, 'I am too deeply committed to science for undiluted faith . . .' Yet it is hard to know exactly where he does stand, for he goes on: 'equally unacceptable to me spiritually is the materialist world of undiluted fact'; while in the same paragraph he comments, 'That Gaia can be both spiritual and scientific is, for me, deeply satisfying'.

I find it hard to understand what James Lovelock, as a scientist, means by 'spiritual' and 'spiritually' here, for the words seem drained of significance outside the religious matrix within which they were conceived, and in our times, for most of us, they are little more than dead metaphors used inexactly for something we would like to think exists, 'ungraspable but important', in the materialist universe we appear to inhabit. Moreover, should the Gaia hypothesis that the Earth itself is a single living organism ever be proved scientifically, then surely it would become an undiluted fact in a materialist world. It is hard to see what 'religious' status 'Gaia' could have then.

In retrospect, James Lovelock's decision to use anthropomorphic language in the books designed to introduce his hypothesis to a wider audience seems doubly unfortunate, for it feeds into the atavistic, and I think phoney, religiosity about the Earth that exists at the fringes of the Green movement, and indeed within orthodox religion itself as this millennium draws to an end, while it cannot have helped the standing of the hypothesis among scientists within whose disciplines 'Gaia' must eventually be proved or disproved.

9

King of the blues, poor man of American poetry

Yes I'm a poor boy today; but tomorrow I may be a big millionaire . . .
(Peetie Wheatstraw, 'Poor Millionaire Blues')

If you look for the work of Robert Johnson in an anthology of American poetry, the chances are that you will be disappointed. Yet he was one of the great poets of the inter-war years. The explanation of this seeming paradox is ready to hand, for as some readers will know, Johnson was a blues singer. Inevitably this means that he has been pigeon-holed as a folk musician, and his poems as folk-song, according to the categories of a dominant Western literary culture.

It may be argued that this is quite correct. After all, Robert Johnson *was* part of a folk tradition and the blues *are* sung to musical accompaniment. However, the definition is also a relegation: it makes an implicit statement about the confines, and therefore the possible achievement, of Johnson's art. This is so because ever since Bishop Percy published his *Reliques of Ancient British Poetry* in 1765, it has been assumed by the majority of educated collectors and students of folk-song that the genre is limited in scope, and that consequently it is inferior by its very nature to the high art which defines culture in bourgeois tradition.

Throughout the nineteenth century and into the twentieth, composers, and to a lesser extent poets, regarded folk music and poetry as a source of inspiration. But it has always been presented as exactly that, a source, to be subsumed into a higher form of artistic expression. This assumption has been so thoroughly internalized, that it even governed white discussions of jazz in the 1940s and 1950s as jazz became more sophisticated and therefore intellectually respectable. So the blues – folk music – was considered important as one of the 'roots' of jazz, but was generally dismissed in a couple of paragraphs with a passing reference to Leadbelly and Blind Lemon Jefferson. In the 1950s, to prefer the blues when you should be listening to Parker and Monk was to tread a decidedly inferior path.

When you turn to the histories of poetry, the blues, again, appears only as an 'influence' on poets like Langston Hughes who, we are told, drew on folk forms to articulate modern black experience. The irony is that Hughes only had a superficial knowledge of the blues, while bluesmen who were his contemporaries – Jefferson, Charley Patton, Little Brother Montgomery, Blind Willie McTell, for example – were already articulating black experience in a poetry which is memorable for its subtlety, wit, emotional range and depth. However, such bluesmen were invisible to the dominant white culture which established the categories and the criteria by which poetry was judged. This is still largely true, even today. In what is otherwise a magisterial survey of English and American poetry, *A History of Modern Poetry*, David Perkins can write of Langston Hughes:

> He boldly exploited the modern freedom of poetic content and form in order to render the life, feelings and speech of people in Harlem. Though his presentation was naturalistic, it was in some ways a sentimental naturalism. Remarkably many of the characters in his poems are whores, gamblers, drug addicts, gangsters, drunks, and the like, so that Hughes's Harlem becomes a lurid place remote from the actual city. The feelings of his protagonists were those implicit in the music on which he based his poetic forms. In jazz pieces they tended to be vital and insouciant and in the blues they tended to be despondent, but in either case they reflected conventions. Nevertheless, Hughes's rendering of contemporary black experience was more realistic and vivid than that of any other poet before or during the 1920s. He looked further into the heart than any other black poet except Toomer, sensitively noting the ambivalences and psychic harms to which blacks are vulnerable in America.

The naïvety, ignorance and (unintentional) condescension of this statement are astounding and, given the fact that it was published in 1976, inexcusable, though I am sure that many whites would read it with no more than a nod of agreement. I shall only comment that the blues, too, is full of references to whores, gamblers, drug addicts, gangsters, drunks 'and the like', and that quite often the singer and the subject of the song are one and the same. Lucille Bogan almost certainly worked part-time as a prostitute, Charley Jordan was a bootlegger who was shot in the spine and became a paraplegic, Tommy Johnson was an alcoholic – yet they were all great blues singers, poets in their own right. Given the nature of black society in America between the wars, there is nothing 'remarkable' in this, nor is Hughes's portrayal of such characters 'lurid' or 'remote' from the actual city. Whores, gamblers, gangsters and drunks were common to black secular society and were often the heroes and heroines of it. Moreover, if Hughes's jazz- and blues-based poems reflect 'conventions', that is because he was drawing on art forms which do not necessarily view convention as a term of dispraise. But the real flaw in Perkins's argument, which opens onto a chasm of ignorance, is his assertion that 'Hughes's rendering of contemporary black experience was more realistic and vivid than that of any other poet before or during the 1920s'. Langston Hughes became visible to whites (and so canonized in literary history) because he conformed to expectations: he 'drew on' folk poetry and music, in the manner established by European Romanticism, to produce a *written*, high art poetry which, by definition, was superior to its oral sources. Langston Hughes made it; he became one of us.

Yet as a poet, compared with Jefferson, Patton, McTell, and dozens of other blues singers, he was second best. One of the great lost opportunities of this century is the fact that no wealthy individual or institution thought it worthwhile to make a complete collection of 78 records in mint condition of blues and gospel music as these streamed out of commercial recording studios from the mid-1920s. Today, such a collection would be a priceless national treasure. Instead, decades after they were issued, many of the great early bluesmen have been saved from oblivion by white enthusiasts knocking on doors and asking after old records; and some of the finest pre-war blues exist on a single, battered (in some cases, barely audible) 78.

~

I came across Robert Johnson in 1956 or 1957 when I obtained a poorly dubbed copy of his 'Preaching Blues' on a bootleg acetate disc. The same year, I read T. S. Eliot for the first time, in a well-produced Faber paperback. I did not understand 'Prufrock' or *The Waste Land* at all, yet I hardly understood 'Preaching Blues' any better. For Johnson and Eliot represented traditions which were equally remote from the culture of the borderland market town where I grew up. Yet when I read in Eliot lines like

> I will show you fear in a handful of dust

or heard Johnson sing

> Well the blues
> > is a achin' old heart disease . . .
> Like consumption
> > killing me by degrees

each had the same powerful emotional hold on me that I have never forgotten, and which has led me back to their work time and again during the past forty years. It did not matter that I did not 'understand' them in 1956; that is, that I could not articulate to myself or anyone else why such lines stirred me, or even what they meant. The experience was sufficient, and if I know more about their lives and work now, if I understand them better, it is none the less because of that initial experience that I return to their poems.

As a poet, Eliot has the reputation of being difficult, and as a man, someone who guarded his privacy. Yet ironically he was far more open to me than Johnson. I could read Eliot's essays, critical studies on him by the score, biographies and in 1988 the first 600-page volume of his letters. There were also dozens of photographs recording every period of his life.

In contrast, apart from two pioneering studies, *The Country Blues* by Samuel Charters (1959) and Paul Oliver's *Blues Fell This Morning* (1960), there was almost no information on the blues at all to give a context to Johnson's song, and I had to wait another six years before I heard more of his blues, when in 1961, Columbia issued an LP with sixteen recordings, following this a few years later with a second album. Together, they made all twenty-nine of his songs available for the first time.

Yet as for Johnson the man, it seemed as if he was possessed of an anonymity so impénetrable that it might have been admired by 'Ole Possum' himself. All that was known for certain were the dates of his recording sessions in San Antonio and Dallas, Texas, in 1936 and 1937, and the year of his death, 1938. For the rest, there was legend and rumour, and scattered anecdotes from ageing bluesmen who had known Johnson in the 1930s. There was not even a photograph, and researchers looking for traces of him in the Delta region of Mississippi, where he was born and spent much of his life, drew a blank.

This only changed when the Texas folklorist Mack McCormick, through a combination of luck and determination, discovered that Johnson was hardly ever known by that name among his family and neighbours. When, however, he started asking after Robert Spencer or R. L. Spencer, he uncovered a whole family network, including Johnson's ex-girlfriend and son. McCormick also claims Johnson used the name Robert Dodds and that he also located a widow and children. According to other informants quoted in an article in *78 Quarterly* by Stephen Calt and Gayle Dean Wardlow, he was also known as Robert Saunders, Robert Dusty and Robert Saxton. While such claims have never been verified, it is clear that Robert Johnson was a difficult man to track down.

In 1976 McCormick announced the imminent publication of a book on Johnson, based on his discoveries, to be called 'Biography of a Phantom', but this seems to have entered the world of mystery and legend surrounding the singer, for it has never appeared. However, in 1989 Peter Guralnick published *Searching for Robert Johnson*,[1] which, as he freely acknowledges, draws heavily on information gained in an extended interview with McCormick. At eighty-two pages, eked out with familiar period photographs from the Library of Congress archives, it only just qualifies as a 'book' and indicates the paucity, still, of our information on Johnson. Another blues researcher, Steve LaVere has announced he is working on a 'definitive' biography, but until it or 'Biography of a Phantom' is published, Guralnick's book casts an invaluable shaft of light on one of the most important and enigmatic figures in blues history.

The year 1989 was fruitful. It also saw the publication in *78*

[1] Published in England by Secker and Warburg, 1990.

Quarterly of two photographs of Johnson, one a studio portrait, the other a dime-store booth photo, both obtained by LaVere from one of Johnson's sisters.[2]

There is no room here to recount Johnson's early life or family history which led to the confusion over names; nor to explain why he is such a pivotal figure in the Delta blues tradition. All of this is documented in *Searching for Robert Johnson* and elsewhere.[3] I want to return to the point I set out to make: that he is a great American poet, unacknowledged as such because he does not fit into the categories of European-American literary culture. Yet I think there is a need to approach this indirectly, through some of the insights provided by Guralnick in his book.

Even before he had learned to play the guitar well, it seems clear that Robert Johnson had determined on a career as a professional bluesman, despite the scorn of older contemporaries like Son House and Willie Brown, from whom he was learning. This meant a rambling, transitory life, and there is evidence that, during the 1930s, he played not only through the Delta, but as far afield as St Louis, Detroit, Chicago and New York. Often he played alone, but sometimes he teamed up with another bluesman, one of whom was Johnny Shines who is an important source for Peter Guralnick. When they arrived in a new town, according to Shines in Guralnick's paraphrase, 'they would play on street corners or in front of the local barber-shop, set up in front of restaurants or in the town square, re-establish some local connection to make a house-rent party in the city or a house-rocking get-back at some plantation shack out from town.' As professionals, they had to play what people wanted, and in some places that might not be the blues. Guralnick reports Shines as recalling that Johnson could sing the latest Bing Crosby hit and

[2] *78 Quarterly*, 4. The studio portrait was reproduced with an earlier version of this essay which appeared in *Planet* 88 (1991). The issue of *78 Quarterly* also contains a biographical article, referred to earlier, by Stephen Calt and Gayle Dean Wardlow which is a no-nonsense debunking of Johnson that does not square with Guralnick's portrait, and to which I do not subscribe.

[3] An LP, *The Roots of Robert Johnson* (Yazoo L-1073), is particularly useful.

could play in many styles, including that of the popular white downhome singer Jimmie Rogers. He seems to have had an effortless knack of picking up any song, any tune.

Sometimes Johnson and Shines found themselves playing no matter what, for the wrong reasons. Guralnick quotes Shines recalling a time when they played for a white audience in a small Illinois town. They were engaged for several nights at a club, and things seemed to be going well. As Shines tells it:

> So Robert starts out playing and me right with him, and they tried to get us to stay there, so we stayed a couple of nights, and the people at that time paid twenty-five cents a head, but we found out that the admission was not for music but to see our skin. You see, they had never seen a coloured man before. We didn't want to be part of a freak sideshow. The guy thought we wanted more money, but we just wanted to get the hell out of there. After all, a man have his pride. What is it to sell his pride for a few pennies?

According to Peter Guralnick, several bluesmen who knew Johnson, remarked on the fact that they never saw him practise, and that he was very jealous of his technique, turning aside to mask his hands if he thought another guitarist was watching him. Guralnick reports that several of Johnson's women friends told Mack McCormick of how 'they would wake up in the middle of the night to discover him fingering the guitar strings almost soundlessly at the window by the light of the moon. If he realised that they were awake, he would stop almost immediately . . .'

What was he like? Peter Guralnick puzzles over this a great deal. Robert Lockwood Jr., Johnson's stepson and a bluesman, described him as a 'loner'. To Johnny Shines he seemed almost 'neutral'. Guralnick quotes the white recording engineer from Johnson's first session as saying, 'In my mind he was a nice little quiet-spoken coloured boy.' Calt and Wardlow, in their *78 Quarterly* article, quote a neighbour, Elizabeth Peterson Moore, as saying that he never mentioned 'anything out of the ordinary in his conversation' and she does not remember him playing any of the blues for which he is now highly regarded.

He had a habit of disappearing suddenly, often for weeks on end, and no one knew where he had been. And Shines, according to Calt and Wardlow, once dismissed him in private conversation as a 'bum who was always getting drunk and pissing in his pants'. This is quoted in Calt and Wardlow's 'deconstruction' of Robert Johnson, and has to be squared with Shines's remembrance of him elsewhere. Guralnick quotes him as recalling: 'His shoulders were carried high with a little pitch forward. His sharp, slender fingers fluttered like a trapped bird . . . The cataract in his left eye was immediately noticeable to anyone.'

The studio portrait of Johnson is interesting in the light of Shines's description. It is a mirror-image of a studio portrait of Big Bill Broonzy, taken about the same time: there are the same shined shoes, smart double-breasted pin-stripe suit; the same flash tie and tie-pin; and while Broonzy wears what looks like a broad-brimmed Borsalino, Johnson sports a snap-brimmed trilby. I think Broonzy, or rather Broonzy's image, of the bluesman as hero, is what Johnson is trying to be: relaxed, smiling, handsome and confident. But for Johnson, the mirror in this photograph is not quite right. His shoulders are carried high, just as Johnny Shines remembered, but they are tensed, and the long fingers that Shines recalled fluttering like a trapped bird just seem trapped in the moment caught in the photograph, sinewed and tensed, clamped against the frets.

As to his face, there is a smile, but it is not the confident charmer's smile projected by Broonzy; it is an uncertain, off-balance smile, and the more you look at it, the less certain you are that it is a smile at all. And the total composition of the face is turned somehow askew by the cataract; his left eye narrowed, the right seeming by comparison unnaturally enlarged and focusing you cannot tell where. It is a fascinating photograph, compared with Broonzy's. The portrait of a man for whom things do not come out right.

Peter Guralnick quotes Mack McCormick, who must have thought about Johnson more than anyone. For all his research and all his knowledge, Johnson remains to him a 'cypher'. Perhaps that is why he has so far failed to publish his book. How can you write the biography of a phantom? Guralnick seems to have come to a not dissimilar conclusion: 'He was well-mannered, he was soft-spoken, he was indecipherable. No one seems to have any idea where the music came from.'

One last image before turning to the songs. Guralnick quotes Johnny Shines on the impact of one of Johnson's most moving blues on an audience in St Louis:

> One time in St Louis we were playing one of the songs that Robert would like to play with someone in a great while, 'Come on in My Kitchen'. He was playing very slowly and passionately, and when we had quit, I noticed no one was saying anything. Then I realised they were crying – both women and men.

Firstly, there is no need to puzzle over Johnson's ordinariness, as Peter Guralnick does, for the poet and the individual are not the same thing. Only a naïve romanticism expects to find the poetry somehow bodied forth in the man, who is more likely to talk about his hypochondria or the importance of good leather shoes than exemplify the flamboyant *poète maudit*. T. S. Eliot went all his life disguised as a banker, yet it is he, not the excessive, extrovert Pound, who wrote *The Waste Land*, that most intensely emotional Modernist poem.

So the person Robert Johnson projects in his songs is an artefact, someone who never was and perhaps could never be, but who touches us, as he touched that audience in St Louis, through the expression of our needs and longings, in a way we never thought possible and which we could never articulate to ourselves. Afterwards, we, like the singer, become ordinary again, but with the experience of the poem as a kind of field of force, an energy reserve of the mind.

Yet still, it might be objected, Robert Johnson was a singer and musician. How can he be mentioned as a poet in the same breath as T. S. Eliot? The roots of poetry in music are well known, though in the West it might seem that we have come a long way from them. Yet I do not think this is so. When we talk of the 'music' of poetry, of its cadence and tone, and when Ezra Pound cast his famous advice in the form of an analogy to music – 'As regarding rhythm: to compose in the sequence of the musical phrase, not in the sequence of the metronome' – these are not empty words or loose analogies, but a recognition that even in written form music is of the essence in poetry. There is still an important sense in which we *hear* poetry and *read* prose.

For a poet in an oral tradition like Johnson, the music that must be implicit in the words on the page in a literary culture unfolds like the multiple petals of a flower in melody, inflections of the voice and in the rhythmic, melodic and tonal nuances of the instrumental accompaniment. It is no accident that in blues tradition, the guitar is often referred to as a 'voice', responding to and echoing the voice of the singer. Aspects of poetry that are condensed in literary tradition are separated out in an oral one – and yet are unified too, in a way that is no less complex or beautiful, and no less valid as poetry because the musical elements are more clearly identifiable as music. For there is a sense in which all poetry aspires to song.

But here lies a problem. You cannot do justice to Johnson in an anthology that only publishes his words. Eliot can be read and his music is apparent. Johnson's must be heard. Moreover, the vocabulary of criticism has been developed in response to written poetry. It is not adequate to handle what are in many ways (ironically) the more complex formal qualities of blues poetry. However, luckily for the literary critic, he is never asked to put this to the test, for high art categories, as I suggested at the beginning, have relegated the blues to an influence on black American poetry; one of its sources, rather than its most important achievement.

In the academies, the blues is studied in departments of ethno-musicology, not literature, and those who profess an interest in American poetry are consequently often unaware of it. As a result, the true history of American poetry this century has never been written.

Johnson had a light, fairly high voice. He sometimes used falsetto to emphasize a line. Almost always he sounded tensed, anxious, hardly ever relaxed. His guitar is the counterpoint of his voice. Though his style of playing is deeply rooted in Delta music, with echoes of Son House, Willie Brown, Charley Patton and others, I have never heard a blues guitar which sounds as Johnson's does, as if it were pitched just at breaking point, where at any moment strings must snap. It is an illusion, no doubt, of his style, but it gives a distinctive signature to his music and adds to that sense of wound-up tautness that is so much a part of his poetry. Sometimes he picks the guitar; sometimes he uses open tuning and a slide. While he may not have been the originator of it, he is also closely associated with the 'walking bass' pattern derived from blues piano.

He recorded on 23, 26 and 27 November 1936, and 19 and 20 June 1937, twenty-nine songs in all. Each was recorded in at least two takes, sometimes three, a standard procedure at the time. Eighteen of these alternative takes are missing; the rest have been published; and in 1990 Columbia brought out a magnificent boxed set of the complete extant recordings in chronological order.[4]

There is no way of knowing who chose the songs and they clearly do not represent the full range of his professional repertoire. Some are derived from singers he knew like Son House, others from the records of bluesmen like Leroy Carr. Some were highly influential on later singers and became standards of the post-war blues. Some of the best are so personal to Johnson that nobody else has attempted them, and they are unlikely to have been a part of his professional repertoire. But all have the stamp of Johnson's artistry which gives his recordings a distinctive unity, and my guess is that the choice of songs was his.

What are the poems about? Certain themes recur relentlessly: the need for love and the fear of it; the sense of betrayal when he is rejected, countered by his own perverse urge to be cruel, which he hardly understands, as if he must create rejection through hurting others in order to be hurt himself:

> When you got a good friend
> > that will stay right by your side . . .[5]
> Give her all of your spare time
> > love and treat her right

---

[4] *Robert Johnson: The Complete Recordings* (LP Columbia C3 46222; CD C467246-2). Blues records are sometimes hard to find. This, the Yazoo album and *78 Quarterly* are readily available from the mail order specialists Red Lick Records, P.O. Box 3, Porthmadoc, Gwynedd.

[5] In blues that use the AAB stanza form, I have omitted the second, repeated line, which is often brilliantly effective when sung, but which can seem flat on the page.

he sings in 'When You Got a Good Friend'. But he cannot take his own advice:

> I mistreated my baby
> > and I can't see no reason why . . .
> Every time I think about it
> > I just wring my hands and cry.

In 'Stones in My Passway' he uses a line that seems as if it comes from an English love ballad:

> I have a bird to whistle
> > and I have a bird to sing . . .

But it is undercut by an unexpected third line:

> I got a woman that I'm lovin'
> > boy, but she don't mean a thing.

In performance, that last line has a mixture of throwaway indifference and bitterness, emphasized by a stylistic signature of Johnson's – a snapped, tremolo note on a bass string after 'loving', which acts as a startling punctuation.

There is a sense in the songs of being hounded, of having to move on, of being betrayed:

> My enemies have betrayed me
> > have overtaken poor Bob at last . . .
> And there's one thing certainly
> > they have stones all in my pass.
> > > ('Stones in My Passway')

In one of his most memorable songs, he borrows the old folk belief in the 'hellhound' as the messenger of death:

> I got to keep movin'
> > I've got to keep movin'
> > blues fallin' down like hail
> > blues fallin' down like hail

> Mmmm mmm mmm mmm
>> blues fallin' down like hail
>> blues fallin' down like hail
> And the day keeps on worryin' me
>> it's a hellhound on my trail
>> hellhound on my trail
>> hellhound on my trail.

Some of the blues are bawdy, playing on images like a phonograph and a needle, a car that will not start, someone else fishing in his pond. But they are not straight, good-time barrel-house songs as they might have been sung by Big Bill and Georgia Tom Dorsey, 'The Hokum Boys'. They are desperate songs, the bawdy transposed by frustration and anger, as in the frenetically performed 'Terraplane Blues':[6]

> Now you know the coils ain't even buzzin'
>> little generator won't get that spark
> Motor's in a bad condition, you gotta have
>> these batteries charged

he sings – before changing suddenly and unexpectedly to a pleading falsetto:

> But I'm cryin' please
>> plea-hease don't do me wrong

then back to normal voice

> Who been drivin' my Terraplane now for
>> you-hoo [falsetto] since I been gone.

Like the Terraplane, nothing in his life works, and he prowls behind the bars of the prison of his aloneness:

> A man is like a prisoner
>> and he's never satisfied

he sings in 'From Four till Late'.

---

[6] The Terraplane was a cheap popular car in the mid-1930s.

'Come on in My Kitchen' expresses this in a complex and unforgettable way. Johnson hums the first two lines of the melody, then sings what is to become the refrain:

> You better come on
> > in my kitchen
> > babe, it's goin' to be rainin' outdoors.

It is a song again about betrayal:

> Ah the woman I love,
> > took from my best friend,
> Some joker got lucky
> > stole her back again . . .

But who has betrayed whom?

> Oh she's gone
> > I know she won't come back
> I taken the last nickel
> > out of her nation sack . . .[7]

In one verse he speaks, rather than sings,

> Oh can't you hear that wind howl'n' all?
> Oh-y', can't you hear that wind would howl?

as the treble strings of the guitar whine in imitation of the wind. In the fifth stanza the betrayal extends beyond his relationship with his lover and his friend, to become universal:

> When a woman gets in trouble
> > everybody throws her down
> Lookin' for her good friend
> > none can be found . . .

---

[7] 'Nation sack' is a shortening of 'donation sack', a pouch used to keep money and valuables.

And the insistent advice or invitation (almost, even, threat) of the refrain is given a new dimension:

> You better come on
> in my kitchen
> baby it's gon' to be rainin' outdoors.

It is an invitation to share, not love, but aloneness, an appeal for, and an offer of, a kind of tenderness, from one to another who knows what it is to be alone. There is no indication that it is accepted, however. The last stanza warns of the hard conditions of winter to come, but the poem ends unresolved and unanswered with the ambiguous refrain, the approach of the storm.

Like many of Johnson's songs, 'Come on in My Kitchen' presents a landscape of the mind for emotions which we find it hard to articulate and perhaps do not want to face. It is not hard to imagine that audience in St Louis and their silent tribute to his art all those years ago.

To the listener the songs give a release, a warrant for our feelings. But for Johnson there appears to have been no release. In 'Cross Road Blues', standing at the crossroads is taken in its literal and symbolic sense:

> I went to the crossroad
> fell down on my knees . . .

he sings in the first stanza,

> Asked the Lord above 'Have mercy now
> save poor Bob if you please.'

I do not think Johnson was a religious man. Gospel music is significantly absent when anybody mentions his repertoire. Here the drama of the sinner appealing for mercy is one in a rapidly changing sequence of images of a desperate inner life:

> Eeeh standin' at the crossroad
> tried to flag a ride . . .
> Didn't nobody seem to know me babe
> everybody passed me by.

A crossroads at dusk in the Delta flatlands can seem one of the loneliest places on Earth, car headlights shimmering towards you along roads that run straight in places for miles on end:

> Standin' at the crossroad baby
> risin' sun goin' down . . .
> I believe to my soul now
> po' Bob is sinkin' down.

The penultimate stanza makes an appeal:

> You can run, you can run
> tell my friend Willie Brown . . .

Willie Brown and his musical partner Son House were the older bluesmen whom in 1930 the teenage Johnson had idolized and from whom he had tried to learn, and who as hardened musicians had mocked his efforts. What should he be told? A kind of confirmation that he was one of them:

> 'at I got the crossroad blues this mornin' Lord
> babe I'm sinkin' down.

The last stanza begins with a visual image of anxiousness, perhaps hope, that is literal and symbolic:

> And I went to the crossroad mama
> I looked east and west . . .

But the anxious looking yields no consolation, affirms the impossibility of love:

> Lord I didn't have no sweet woman
> ooh-well babe in my distress.

It now seems certain from evidence adduced in *Searching for Robert Johnson* that he was murdered when he was playing with another bluesman, David 'Honeyboy' Edwards, at a juke joint in a hamlet, Three Forks, fifteen miles from Greenwood, Leflore

County, Mississippi. The murderer was the jealous proprietor of
the bar, who slipped Johnson a pint of poisoned whiskey.

Robert Johnson died some days later in the rooming house in
Greenwood where he had been staying. He was twenty-seven.
The county police do not seem to have investigated the killing. It
is unlikely that there was an autopsy, for across the section of the
death certificate which requires details of cause of death, whoever
filled out the form has simply written 'No Doctor'. To the county
police in Leflore in 1938 it was just another Darktown killing.

Robert Johnson was probably buried in an unmarked grave in a
black graveyard (for even the dead were segregated), next to the
Little Zion Church a few miles north of Greenwood.

> You may bury my body
> > down by the highway side . . .

Johnson sang in 'Me and the Devil Blues', mumbling as an aside,
'Baby, I don't care where you bury my body when I'm dead and
gone' –

> So my old evil spirit
> > can catch a Greyhound bus and ride.

'Time the destroyer is time the preserver', mused T. S. Eliot in
'Dry Salvages' in *Four Quartets*, remembering the Mississippi
River as it flowed past his childhood home of St Louis. A
generation after he left it, it had become one of the great blues
cities of America, with residents like Peetie Wheatstraw and
Charley Jordan, Henry Townsend and J. D. Short, and itinerant
bluesmen like Robert Johnson and Johnny Shines. But Eliot
would never have heard of them, even had he stayed in St Louis.
For to a man of his class and poetic aspirations, they would have
been invisible.

Time the destroyer is time the preserver,
Like the river with its cargo of dead negroes, cows and chicken coops,
The bitter apple and the bite in the apple.

10

Realpolitik *and Utopia*

The first issue of *Planet*, published in 1970, contained an article by Dafydd Iwan, 'What I Understand by Conservation'. The year 1970 had been designated 'European Conservation Year' and amid all the hype that accompanies the Year of This and the Year of That in mass society, Dafydd Iwan argued that conservation should mean more than a concern for the natural environment. It should mean concern for our cultural environment too, and nowhere more so than in Wales where economic decline, emigration, the influx of English second-home owners and retirees, and the intrusion of a powerful mass media seemed poised in 1970 to force Welsh-language culture towards what might be its last crisis. Dafydd Iwan was in no doubt, therefore, where the priorities lay. As he put it,

> rubbish dumps may be cleared, tips planted with evergreens, fences repaired and wardens employed to keep an eye on picnickers and ramblers, caravans may be screened by artificial hillocks and pylons demolished, but let us not pretend that this alone is doing anything more than applying a cosmetic to the outer skin of a body which is in need of an emergency blood transfusion and a major operation if it is to have any hope of survival.

It was this perception of immediate crisis that impelled many of the best young minds of the late 1960s and 1970s into the language movement. If the environment figured in people's calculations, it was a secondary problem, which as Dafydd Iwan suggested, could be easily tackled by a clean-up operation and some landscaping, all of which could be put on hold while the cultural crisis was resolved.

This single-mindedness of purpose brought results. In his 1970 article, Dafydd Iwan listed Welsh-medium secondary schools, a Welsh-language television channel and radio frequencies as urgent priorities. Today they seem a natural part of the fabric of our culture.

But that divorce between the cultural and the natural environment was – it can be seen now – too easily made. Partly this was so because at the beginning of the seventies the human impact on the Earth was still poorly understood and generally underestimated. As a consequence, 'conservation' to most people meant little more than installing double glazing, demanding bottle banks and saving the panda. Today environmental problems are understood to include rising concentrations of 'greenhouse' gases in the atmosphere with possible global warming as a consequence, large-scale rainforest loss and desertification of marginal farmland, human-induced species extinction on a scale comparable only with the great mass extinctions of the geological past, ozone layer depletion at the poles, and towering above everything, the exponential growth of the human population.

These problems are essentially interactive and global and they are not going to go away. If they cannot be addressed as a matter of urgency and solutions found and acted upon within the next couple of generations, then the specifics of individual cultures will dwindle to insignificance in the general ecological and human population collapse that is likely to occur.

One of our best hopes is that science and technology can be used to help avert such a disaster. After all, the exponential growth of scientific knowledge in a wide array of disciplines in the past two decades is the main reason that we have such a good general understanding of the problems in the first place. Whether or not this will be the case, however, depends entirely on the values of the society in which science and technology operate.

This is one of the contentions of an important book published in 1992, *Beyond the Limits*, by Donella H. Meadows, Dennis L.

Meadows and Jørgen Randers.[1] Two of the authors, Donella Meadows and Dennis Meadows, are systems analysts, and Jørgen Randers is a business analyst. On the basis of their respective disciplines they argue that if society could be persuaded that it wanted sustainability rather than growth, then this could be achieved, even comparatively quickly, through technological and market forces that are already in operation. The need, they claim, is to change the structure of the system in accordance with systems theory:

> In systems terms changing structure means changing the *information* links in a system: the content and timeliness of the data that actors in the system have to work with, and the goals, incentives, costs and feedbacks that motivate or constrain behaviour. The same combination of people, institutions, and physical structures can behave completely differently, if its actors can see a good reason for doing so and if they have the freedom to change.

The problem unfortunately is that at the moment we do not possess that freedom to change because the vast majority of people, from politicians down, remain convinced that the only real solution to economic and social problems is growth. Sticking 'green' or 'sustainable' in front of the word – as many of our would-be political leaders did in the 1992 general election campaign – may have given the electorate the cosy feeling that 'things are being done', but at best the politicians meant by it amelioration (that is to say delaying collapse not averting it) and at worst, nothing. Growth has been and remains a dogma of the industrial system. Consequently, as the authors of *Beyond the Limits* observe,

> the idea that there might be limits to growth is for many people impossible to imagine. Limits are politically unmentionable and economically unthinkable. The society tends to assume away the possibility of limits by placing a profound faith in the powers of technology and the workings of a free market.

[1] *Beyond the Limits: Global Collapse or a Sustainable Future* (Earthscan, 1992).

However, while technology may be able to correct some of the problems created by the present system in the short term, it is highly unlikely that it will be able to do so for long. Based on the evidence of their computer model, World3, which they have been running for twenty years, the Meadows and Jørgen Randers believe that a key factor is likely to be failure of the growth-orientated system to keep pace with ever-increasing levels of the stresses placed upon it, even though (and in fact partly because) it will be successful in curbing some of them temporarily:

> *Time* is in fact the ultimate limit in the World3 model – and, we believe, in the 'real world'. The reason that growth, and especially exponential growth, is so insidious is that it shortens time for effective action. It loads stress on a system faster and faster, until coping mechanisms that have been able to deal with slower rates of change finally begin to fail.

This is also the ultimate limiting factor on the human population which has grown exponentially since the early years of the Industrial Revolution (see graph on p.127). From 1968 to 1992 the population grew from 3.5 to 5.5 billion. The rate of growth has fallen in the past twenty-five years from 2.0 to 1.7 per cent but remains exponential. The Earth's human population on current trends will have doubled to *c.* 10 billion by 2050. (Some population models suggest that this is an underestimate, and that the figure will be closer to 12.5 billion.)[2]

This unchecked growth in one species is *the* major cause of current environmental degradation and the biggest stumbling block in the path of efforts to find solutions. As sociobiologist Edward O. Wilson recently put it: 'The raging monster upon the land is population growth. In its presence, sustainability is but a fragile theoretical construct.'[3]

[2] See, for example, Marguerite Holloway, 'Population pressure', *Scientific American* (September 1992); Henry C. Tuckwell and James A. Koziol, 'World population', *Nature* (17 September 1992); 'Population growth, resource consumption, and a sustainable world', joint communiqué of the Royal Society and the National Academy of Sciences (27 February 1992); and Meadows, Meadows and Randers, *Beyond the Limits*, esp. pp. 23–32.

[3] Edward O. Wilson, *The Diversity of Life* (Allen Lane/Penguin, 1993).

Yet politicians and even many environmentalists have been notoriously reluctant to address the population crisis. There are a number of reasons for this. About 90 per cent of the anticipated growth in the next fifty years will take place in Third World countries where intervention on population control by the industrialized nations is often treated with suspicion. But contraception, and especially abortion, are subjects of fierce dispute in the industrialized nations too, so that opposition from the Roman Catholic Church, the 'pro-life' lobby and even some elements in the feminist movement has placed a significant restraint on Western governments' reaction to population control. In 1985, for example, George Bush cut all American funding to the United Nations Population Fund as well as financial support for international family planning action which in any way counselled or implemented abortion services. Bill Clinton has promised to reverse US policy, but it remains to be seen whether he can do so in the face of the strong anti-abortion lobby in the States.

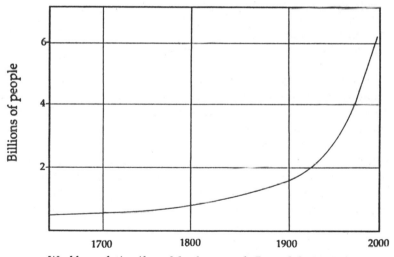

World population (from Meadows *et al.*, *Beyond the Limits*)

The situation is compounded by a tendency in the West to see population as only, or essentially, a Third World problem. Many European countries have in recent decades stabilized their populations and in one or two cases even reduced them. This

127

should give no cause for complacency, however. Countries that have achieved zero population growth are also amongst the world's richest. A certain level of material wealth and population control go hand in hand. But in the production of that wealth, the industrialized nations have placed as much stress on the environment as impoverished Third World countries have done. If a Western level of material wealth is essential to breaking out of the poverty-population trap, then the environment and with it the human species will suffer a collapse long before a significant portion of the Third World comes anywhere near a Western standard of living.

Those who think otherwise are deceiving themselves. To quote Edward O. Wilson again:

> It is . . . sophistic to point to the Netherlands and Japan, as many commentators incredibly still do, as models of densely populated but prosperous societies. Both are highly specialized industrial nations dependent on massive imports of natural resources from the rest of the world. If all nations held the same number of people per square mile, they would converge in quality of life to Bangladesh rather than to the Netherlands and Japan, and their irreplaceable natural resources would soon join the seven wonders of the world as scattered vestiges of an ancient history.

The overwhelming question is what we can do now to avert collapse sometime in the next century – collapse which will no doubt manifest itself in detail in ways we have not foreseen, but which is understood well in broad outline.

Books like *Beyond the Limits* and *The Diversity of Life* are excellent at description and analysis of environmental problems and at warning of the consequences if current trends continue. But when their authors try to draw up a blueprint for effective change they almost always make a sudden transition from the world as it is to utopia. The authors of *Beyond the Limits*, for example, give their version of how a society would think if it was committed to sustainability:

> A sustainable society would be interested in qualitative development, not physical expansion. It would use material growth as a considered tool, not as a perpetual mandate. It would be neither for nor against growth, rather it would begin to discriminate kinds of growth and

purposes for growth. Before this society would decide on any specific growth proposal, it would ask what the growth is for, and who would benefit, and what it would cost, and how long it would last, and whether it could be accommodated by the sources and sinks of the planet. A sustainable society would apply its values and its best knowledge of the earth's limits to choose only those kinds of growth that would actually serve social goals and enhance sustainability. And when any physical growth had accomplished its purposes, it would be brought to a stop.

But how are we to bridge the gulf that exists between utopia and *Realpolitik*? The vision of the Meadows and Jørgen Randers assumes goodwill, peaceableness, reason and love of justice as essential common bonds between nations and among individuals. It takes no account of the world as it is, with political structures geared to self-interest, short-term goals, confrontation, often tyrannical, ruthless and illogical – the confused mosaic of contemporary politics where statesmen make their decisions. In the world of *Realpolitik* politicians have shown time and again their unwillingness to come to terms with the global crisis and to gear our political, economic and social structures to long-term planning. Partly this is the result of culpable ignorance on the part of those who rule us concerning even fundamental environmental problems.

But it is also the product of severe limitations that are built into the democratic system of government. In this system because politicians are periodically dependent on the 'will' of the electorate at four- or five-year intervals, those in power and those seeking power are unlikely to react to environmental crises until the situation is so bad that it is evident to everyone, which in environmental terms is likely to mean too late. Politicians will do almost anything to avoid policies which might involve across-the-board restrictions on the electorate's pursuit of material wealth. (The present British government's policies towards such groups as the unemployed are not a counter example to this because the category is not perceived by it as being of sufficient *electoral* importance.) The democracies, in other words, are caught in a rigid lock-step: power means short-term policies to retain, or gain, the vote of a consumerism-directed electorate.

Under these conditions there is no point in looking to the politicians for leadership. If we are to instigate change that is real and necessary before it is too late, it must be because individuals in their millions come to wish it. The authors of *Beyond the Limits* recognize this. They also recognize that the democratic system in mass society operates against what amounts to a revolutionary vision of this kind:

> The world's leaders have lost the habit of learning and the freedom to learn. Somehow a cultural system has evolved that assigns most people to the role of followers, who expect leaders to have all the answers, and assigns a few people to the role of leaders, who pretend they have all the answers. This perverse system does not allow the development of either leadership capability in the people or learning capability in the leaders.

Yet we *are* an extraordinary species. Our evolutionary development as intelligent, bipedal generalists gave us a unique advantage and led to our rapid spread throughout the habitable regions of the Earth. Our adaptability could, possibly, be a key to our salvation and the reversal of our current drive towards environmental catastrophe. It could, in systems terms, enable us to change the 'information links' in our immensely complex agglomerate of societies.

But it is also possible that our evolved status as highly adaptable generalists has created a genetically-based trap for the species which will allow us to adapt – over a short but crucial time-span in the next fifty years – to deteriorating conditions. We can as easily accept a narrowing of our horizons, so that pollution, water shortage, global warming come to seem 'natural' to most of us. And perhaps we are more readily capable of adapting to the environment in this way through a kind of inertia reinforced by the structures of mass democratic society, than we are to taking the much more difficult path of changing our patterns of behaviour radically, and now, in order to reverse our disastrous impact on nature – an impact which is still far from apparent to the majority of people.

This is the crucial choice that has to be made by each of us as individuals – action or inaction – if we are to retain anything of what might be called human dignity. It is possible that this choice is not a real one in that, although the human mind can perceive the options, our evolutionary history has placed severe restraints on our ability to follow one course rather than another. Yet again, we have come a long way since 1970, in knowledge and understanding if not in any decisive and coherent forms of action. If there are evolved limits on our ability to choose and so to act, it will be our species' tragedy. Either way, we can only find out by trying.

11

At the zoo

Recently I went to Copenhagen Zoo to see its new tropical house. A walkway took me through a 'rain forest' of dense foliage where hundreds of gaily coloured butterflies flitted among flowering bushes. There were humming birds and kingfishers and the humped shape of a sloth high in a tree. A waterfall fed a fast stream that emptied into a pool, where forest ducks floated like toys and water rails padded and plodded on their outsize feet. Invisible loudspeakers emitted a cacophony of shrieks, whistles, burblings, screams and yells. The experience was 'educational' in the way that is considered essential by every gallery and museum these days, and I am resistant to being educated. None the less I enjoyed being in the same space as so many birds and butterflies and so close to them.

But to get there I had had to pass two other enclosures in the same building that were not quite cages but were certainly not 'environments' like the area of contrived rain forest I had come to see. Here, separated from visitors by thick panes of glass were the concrete houses of the gorillas and chimpanzees.

The gorillas were lethargic. One sat on the floor holding a branch of shrivelled leaves in its hand, plucking them and stuffing them in its mouth in a desultory way. Near the glass a mother stood moulding something over and over in her hands. Her baby reached up on tiptoe and tried to pull her hands down to see what it was, its eyes full of curiosity. For a long time the mother ignored it, kneading and moulding whatever it was in her large leathery-black hands, until at last she gave in, letting her left hand fall to her side while she held out the right, palm up for the infant to see. What she held was a bulging green bolus of her own faeces. The child stretched up, one hand holding onto the rim of her palm, face at palm height, inspecting this. The mother looked toward us beyond the glass, though with no obvious interest. There was nothing discernible in the intense black of her eyes set in the black polished face.

It made me uncomfortable and I moved on to the next glassed-in area where a family of chimpanzees formed an immediate contrast. There an old grey-haired male was standing close up to the glass looking curiously at the visitors. At the back, on a concrete dais, a mother cradled a baby, watched by the dominant male. In the middle of the enclosure was an area of boulders and the trunks and lower branches of two dead trees with ropes for swinging. A young chimp, female I think, sat on a branch of one of the trees watched by a mischievous young male sitting behind and above her in the other tree. Suddenly he reached up, seized a rope and swung over the female, banging her on the head with his feet, to land high in her tree in the midst of an explosion of angry calls and jeering screams. The female chased him down – more screams – and the young male knuckle-walked round the pile of boulders back up into his own tree, above and behind the female again. After more jeering and threatening they appeared to lose interest in each other, but when the female turned away, the male seized the rope again, swung over the female and banged her on the head before landing in her tree once more. More screams, and this time tree-shaking, head-twisting, arm-flailing.

The dominant male turned from watching the mother and baby, clambered down from the dais and chased the young male vigorously round the boulders back up into its tree. The two looked at each other silently for a while and then the dominant male knuckle-walked back to the dais with a distinct swagger of his immense muscled shoulders. Chimpanzees are very power-ful and in a rage can tear off the arm of a man. The dominant male could easily have caught the young chimp if he had wanted to, but he was only asserting his authority, warning him off.

Back on the dais the dominant male took the baby from its mother, placed it on its back and pushed it gently away from him by holding its spindly uplifted arms. Then towards him. Back and forth in a game. After a spell of this he did a slow handstand against the wall, pouting down with his lips as the baby reached up to touch his face, only to be diverted by more screams of rage, more banging and flailing from the jeering male and the infuriated young female. The big chimpanzee slowly walked his feet down to the floor, left the baby to its mother and perched on the edge of the dais, looking intently and silently at the trouble-making male, the power tensed in the muscles of his great bowed shoulders.

In Western culture we still operate with the notion of our uniqueness. When pressed, we have to concede that we are animals – but such different animals. Partly this is an inheritance from the Judaeo-Christian tradition which emphasizes the separate creation of humankind by God. That view is no longer tenable, but it in its turn must have derived from the development of a fully human consciousness in early *Homo sapiens* a hundred thousand years or so ago, when sense impressions, emotions and proto-thought fused into the illumination of self-awareness. We still bear within us what might be termed that ur-sensibility. It is the core of our identity as a conscious species and it is being reinforced today by the exponential development of machine-civilization which has created the not-nature which we inhabit and where we feel at home. Nature in our world is increasingly elsewhere, remote from civilized life. We feel curious about it at times and enjoy nature films; we make expeditions into it for picnics or white-water canoeing; but we do not live in it, nor do we wish to.

In effect we have created on Earth the scenario from science fiction in which colonists on an alien planet isolate themselves in sealed cities from a hostile environment. The city is where nearly all of us live today even if, notionally, our house is in the countryside. We communicate by telephone, fax, or the Internet. If we have to meet someone we travel in the sealed unit of our car along tarmac roads and concrete superhighways. We have made ourselves as remote from nature as we can. No other creature has done this: we are, our civilization tells us, unique.

Yet while science has created the base for the technology which reinforces in such powerful ways the human feeling of uniqueness, it has also over the past 200 years eroded any possible theoretical foundation for such a feeling in at least three important ways.

First, it has pushed the history of our species back into what even 150 years ago would have seemed an improbably remote past. *Homo sapiens*, we now know, emerged as a fully evolved species 100,000 years ago, while *Homo sapiens* features can be seen emerging in the fossil record for at least 100,000 years before that – far beyond the 4004BC that was widely held by theologians in Darwin's time to be the date of the Creation.

But the revolution in palaeoanthropology that has taken place this century has opened up a deeper and more intriguing view of our history. Our genus Homo is now peopled with ancestor species, *Homo erectus* and *Homo habilis*, that take us back to at least 2.1 million years ago; and before them, in the human family Hominidae, the Australopithecines, a complex array that includes *A. boisei*, *A. robustus*, *A. africanus* and *A. afarensis*, and which takes us back to *c.* 5 million years ago – a scale of time that our brains are not adequate to imagine in any meaningful way.

In this sense alone we are not unique but part of an evolving hominid family. A get-out for uniqueness might be the fact that we are the only surviving hominid species and therefore should be considered the pinnacle of our biological family. However, we should be wary when the evaluator places himself at the pinnacle of anything – it is too easy and smacks too readily of self-serving, as Europeans should be aware from their history of colonization in the modern era. Moreover, to view evolution in this way is to misunderstand it, something biologists are forever telling us but which it seems so convenient to forget. For evolutionary trends do not encode any kind of value judgement. Evolution is not 'leading to' something – refining life so that today's species (including our own) are superior to those of the past. Rather, speciation is the result of the constant random adaptation of living organisms to changing conditions over immense periods of time with no goal other than survival.

One last point: for 70,000 years we were not unique even in our own time, for *Homo sapiens* shared the Earth with the Neanderthals who were either a subspecies (*Homo sapiens neanderthalensis*) or a full species (*Homo neanderthalensis*). Their range stretched throughout Europe to the Near East where they were the dominant hominid for *c.* 90,000 years until 30,000 years ago when they became extinct. There is ambiguous evidence that Neanderthals may have interbred with *Homo sapiens* (hence in part the debate over their status as a species), but either way they were very different from us – stocky and powerfully built, with large brains and distinctive facial features. We shall probably never know how modern humans and Neanderthals reacted to each other; the only (as yet inconclusive) evidence is that at some locations they may have interbred. But a crucial barrier between them may well have been the likelihood that Neanderthals lacked the ability for complex speech – either because of anatomical and brain differentiation from *H. sapiens* or because they had not evolved a culture that *required* complex speech (like so much about the Neanderthals this is a matter of much speculation amongst palaeoanthropologists). Their contemporaries, our ancestors, certainly did possess complex speech at this time, however, and it is hard not to feel that this would have acted as an alienating barrier between the two groups, who would have competed for territory and resources as *Homo sapiens* expanded into the Near East and Europe.

The second way in which science has eroded humankind's traditional assumption of uniqueness is an outgrowth of the first, for we now know that the hominid family to which we belong is part of the superfamily of the Hominoidea that includes the gibbons and the great apes (the chimpanzees, gorillas and orang-utans). We are not descended from the apes, as Darwin's clerical opponents mocked, but we are closely related to them, sharing a common ancestor at *c.* 6 million years ago. A measure of the closeness of that relationship is the 98 per cent of genes which modern humans have in common with the two species of chimpanzee.

The third inroad of science relates to the discovery that all living cells use DNA as their self-replicating genetic material. All forms of life including our own consequently share one of their most fundamental aspects, an inheritance from the beginnings of life in the early oceans over 3.5 billion years ago. We have hardly begun to absorb the philosophical implications, but this insight into life's structure must counter once and for all the Judaeo-Christian emphasis on humankind's uniqueness, as ideas derived from genetics seep into the general culture.

~

We have been fascinated with chimpanzees ever since Europeans encountered them during their exploration of the west coast of Africa at the beginning of the modern era. From the start it was recognized that they bore a remarkable resemblance to humans, even though they seemed grotesque in the eyes of most observers. That resemblance fed into a racist mythology that was being forged in the sixteenth century and used to justify the slave trade. For though chimpanzees (it was thought) certainly did not resemble whites, they did reside in the same region as West African blacks. And were not chimpanzees notoriously libidinous, as were blacks? There was a widely held belief that chimpanzees coupled with black women given the opportunity. And black men – as slave-owners declared in the *ante-bellum* South and as white supremacists asserted for a long time after the Civil War – have an inordinate lust for white women. The circle was never quite closed on the relationship of chimpanzees and black humans – but it hovered as a dark thought at the edge of European racist belief.

It was a depressing tangle of lies and ignorance but it is significant that Europeans could not erase from their minds the haunting resemblance of chimpanzees to humans, even if they distanced their own white kind by interposing West African blacks. But that resemblance has always been an uncomfortable one for those brought up on the Bible, whether they were racist or not. For the chimpanzee is like a mocking image in a hall of mirrors if you believe yourself to be made in the image of God. So many gestures, especially facial gestures, and the eyes, are like our own, and yet when looked at without understanding chimpanzee behaviour can seem erratic, irrational and unpredictable – sometimes like an unruly child, but at others starkly animal and 'non-human'.

No wonder that Christians opposed Darwin after the publication of *The Origin of Species* (1859) and *The Descent of Man* (1871) which drew out the implications of his theory for our own species; or that cartoonists should caricature him as an ape. Not only did the theory of evolution remove the ground from under the theologians, as Darwin foresaw; it was also the beginning of the challenge of science to our feeling of human apartness, the undermining of that unique pinnacle on which we thought we stood.

Now we know immensely more about the chimpanzees, our nearest living relative. We know that they use tools regularly: they fish for termites by dipping grass stems or small twigs into openings in nests. They select stones which are used as hammers to crush open intractable nuts. They can co-ordinate social behaviour to plan hunting expeditions for monkeys and are able to share food. And as one extraordinary series of incidents observed by Jane Goodall at Gombe in Tanzania suggests, they are capable of engaging in what can only be called proto-warfare: after the chimpanzees under her observation had divided into two groups, each occupying a separate territory, the larger group began sending out small raiding parties which over a period of time set upon and killed individuals from the smaller group until the group was extirpated.

Chimpanzee tool use is still very primitive, but probably not so different from that of the earliest Australopithecines: stone tools in each case are simple eoliths, stones selected by size, shape and weight for a particular task, but not retouched or refashioned in any way. There is a huge gap between such a culture and the primitively shaped tools fashioned by *Homo habilis* (and just possibly by his contemporary *Australopithecus robustus*).

A major limiting factor in chimpanzee development, as it must have been for our early hominid ancestors, is that the species is not capable of articulate speech for physiological reasons. But research this century has shown that chimpanzees are capable of abstract thinking, as well as the manipulation of sign language and other systems that do not depend on speech.

At one level the gap between us and them is small – we share 98 per cent of their genes. At another, when comparing our cultures, it is huge, and it is fascinating to reflect that this appears to be the result of a mere 2 per cent difference in our genetic make-up.

I had gone to Copenhagen Zoo after reading the books listed below. I had gone there to see the 'rain forest', but it is the chimpanzees that keep recurring in my mind – how watching their behaviour, and understanding it in the light of what I had read, has changed my perception of them and of ourselves, and how looking into their eyes it was hard not to feel that I was taking a look deep into our own.

Postscript

This essay is indebted to the following works: *The Cambridge Encyclopedia of Human Evolution* (Cambridge University Press, 1992); Jared Diamond, *The Rise and Fall of the Third Chimpanzee* (Vintage, 1991); Eugene D. Genovese, *Roll, Jordan, Roll: The World the Slaves Made* (André Deutsch, 1975); Jane Goodall, *The Chimpanzees of Gombe: Patterns of Behaviour* (The Belknap Press, Harvard University Press, 1986); Winthrop D. Jordan, *The White Man's Burden: Historical Origins of Racism in the United States* (Oxford University Press, 1974); Richard G. Klein, *The Human Career: Human Biological and Cultural Origins* (University of Chicago Press, 1989); W. C. McGrew, *Chimpanzee Material Culture: Implications for Human Evolution* (Cambridge University Press, 1992); John Reader, *Missing Links: The Hunt for Earliest Man* (1981; 2nd edn Penguin, 1988); G. Philip Rightmire, *The Evolution of Homo Erectus* (Cambridge University Press, 1990); Christopher Stringer and Clive Gamble, *In Search of the Neanderthals* (Thames and Hudson, 1993); Erik Trinkhaus and Pat Shipman, *The Neanderthals: Changing the Image of Mankind* (Jonathan Cape, 1993).

12

A walk along Corsons Inlet

> I went for a walk over the dunes again this morning
> to the sea,
> then turned right along
>   the surf
>
>   round a naked headland
>   and returned
>
>   along the inlet shore:

It might be the beginning of a diary poem, another gloss in the margins of late Romanticism. But a 'walk' with A. R. Ammons is entirely different – the poem the medium for an energized restlessness that shifts constantly between the fluid forms and motions of nature and those of the mind, between sharply focused detail and reflections that are philosophical but which refuse to run aground as philosophy.

    In the walk enacted in 'Corsons Inlet' Ammons is 'released from forms', from the categories that bind and stifle us when we try to think in conventional terms, instead of freeing our thoughts to see where they go:

>   you can find
>   in my sayings
>   swerves of action
>   like the inlet's cutting edge:
>   there are dunes of motion,

organizations of grass, white sandy paths of remembrance
in the overall wandering of mirroring mind:

The dynamics of nature mirrors the dynamics of the mind, and
we should go with this, refusing Western culture's insistence on
ultimate, subsuming categories:

> . . . Overall is beyond me: is the sum of these events
> I cannot draw, the ledger I cannot keep, the accounting
> beyond the account:

Nature and the mind possess order, but it is order within flow,
provisional and constantly changing, at least as far as we can
perceive it. Where are the straight lines and divisions in nature?

> manifold events of sand
> change the dune's shape that will not be the same shape
> tomorrow,

and it is the same with the mind, if we are attentive to its
directions:

> so I am willing to go along, to accept
> the becoming
> thought, to stake off no beginnings or ends, establish
>   no walls:

This is immediately apparent in A. R. Ammons's forms that are
patterned but not structured in a predictable way. Ammons is an
inheritor of William Carlos Williams and shares that poet's
suspicion of European culture's tradition of formal stanzas and
metres (which in Ammons's terms are a product of a constricting
notion of mind). In an interview published in *The Manhattan
Review* Ammons commented on his stanza forms:

> In some [of my poems], the indentations correspond from stanza to
> stanza, the same line by line. But in some of them there is the random.
> I usually feel that I don't have anything to say of my own until I have
> tripped the regular world, until I have thrown the Western mind itself
> somehow off, and I think that's what those – if I began to write a

sonnet, for example, I think I would be stultified and silenced by that form, because it's my nature to want to trip that form out of existence as a way of making room for myself to speak and act.[1]

For the same reason, Ammons breaks down conventional punctuation, avoiding capitals and full stops as much as possible. He refers to this in the same interview as a kind of democratization of language, based on a feeling 'that the world is so interpenetrated that it must be one tissue of size, of letters'.

A characteristic of Ammons's punctuation is his substitution of the colon for the full stop. Language to him is a kind of 'geometrical or topological surface like terrain, or "landscapes" which is a very strong word in my poetry'. And landscapes, as in 'Corsons Inlet', are interpenetrative and dynamic:

> So the colon jump should do that, just connect and connect and connect, until you build not just the assertion you're making but this landscape.
>
> I've never been interested in single discursive statements as such, as explanation, but I'm interested in clusters of those, because then they become, they sort of come to be the thing they represent. They're many-sided.

In 'Corsons Inlet',

<pre>
            the news to my left over the dunes and
    reeds and bayberries was
            fall: thousands of tree swallows
            gathering for flight:
            an order held
            in constant change: a congregation
    rich with entropy: nevertheless, separable, noticeable
            as one event,
                    not chaos: preparations for
    flight from winter,
    cheet, cheet, cheet, cheet, wings rifling the green clumps,
    beaks
</pre>

[1] Interview in *The Manhattan Review*, vol. 1, no. 2 (1980). 'Corsons Inlet' is most readily available in A. R. Ammons, *The Selected Poems (Expanded Edition)* (W. W. Norton, 1986).

at the bayberries
a perception full of wind, flight, curve,
sound:
the possibility of rule as the sum of rulelessness:
the 'field' of action
with moving, incalculable center:

Form here mirrors the event as perceived by mind and mediated
by language. Words can never be the same as the event (though
they can be an event in themselves), but insofar as words are an
attribute of mind, and mind mirrors nature in its motions, words
can be used to create in the mind something which comes very
close to the provisional, flowing nature of the event. Referring to
another poem, 'Motion', Ammons said in the *Manhattan Review*
interview:

> I was trying to deal with the difference between words and things. I
> was trying to insist that somehow, although there was no direct
> contact between words and things, the motion of mind and thought
> corresponded to natural motions, meanders, you know, the winds or
> streams. And that these might be parallel motions and where a level
> at which the representation was so basic and so close that it was
> nearly like actuality itself.

Ammons was raised on a farm in a poor community in North
Carolina during the Depression. Later he graduated in science.
These two aspects of his experience act on each other in the
poems, that delight in observation of detail which transforms
through colon'd sentences into different orders of more abstract
perception and back again. Ammons does not write consciously
as someone trained in science. As he says in the interview, when
he began writing he was also studying for his degree: 'I was
never aware that I was writing poetry with scientific termino-
logy, I was just writing from where I was, which was a mixture of
science and poetry.'

None the less, science underwrites the poems in an important
way:

> It seems to me that the pagan tradition is now represented by science.
> Of course, there have to be modifications, but if you think of the

pagan societies as rather carefully paying attention to what the natural forces were around them and then trying to identify with and, as it were, listen to what that force was and appease it, and know something about it, learn its nature, then science does precisely the same thing today.

Science 'puts aside, for the moment, its personal interest in things and tries to know what is the nature of things out there'. By contrast, the humanities

often feel opposed to that because that attitude obviously puts human things secondary, whereas the humanities have often claimed that man is the center of everything and has the right to destroy or build or do whatever he wishes. Well, that's an exaggerated statement – just to put it briefly.

Compare the lines from 'Corsons Inlet' about the tree swallows with this:

> Mark how the feathered tenants of the flood,
> With grace of motion that might scarcely seem
> Inferior to angelical, prolong
> Their curious pastime! shaping in mid air
> (And sometimes with ambitious wing that soars
> High as the level of the mountain-tops)
> A circuit ampler than the lake beneath –
> Their own domain; but ever, while intent
> On tracing and retracing that large round,
> Their jubilant activity evolves
> Hundreds of curves and circlets, to and fro,
> Upward and downward, progress intricate
> Yet unperplexed, as if one spirit swayed
> Their indefatigable flight . . .

This is the opening of Wordsworth's 'Water-Fowl' which like 'Corsons Inlet' is concerned with form and motion in nature. In fact in Wordsworth's fascination with the wheeling, restless flight of the birds, the 'tracing and retracing', the

> Hundreds of curves and circlets, to and fro,
> Upward and downward

there is an embryo Ammons poem waiting to mature.

But it cannot. It is weighted with a humanist tradition that must, as Ammons says, centre everything in man. The language occasionally breaks loose, or almost loose, as in the lines isolated above, but they operate against a powerful undertow. The birds are 'feathered tenants', their motion almost 'angelical', their flight around the lake 'a curious pastime', as they surge up on 'ambitious' wing, and so on. And though a sense of the birds' restless energy is conveyed, it is inhibited by Wordsworth's choice of form, the classical ten-syllable line based on the iamb that has dominated English verse since the sixteenth century.

I like 'Water-Fowl'. Almost despite itself it rises above the artifices of diction of eighteenth-century rural verse, but incompletely, like the form of a sculpture only half-released from the stone. But crucially it lacks Ammons's sense of the conformity of motion in nature with that of the human mind. Wordsworth's observer is static, a fixed point in the scene, the shape of words formed in an ordered consciousness to an end already known. Ammons will have none of this:

> I may have said somewhere, but I still think it's true, that you don't want the poem to amount to no more than you already knew when you began to write. Whatever kind of instrument it may be, it must be one capable of churning up what you didn't already know. That's what creativity is, and it is to be surprised by the end of the poem as much as you expect the reader to be surprised. That's why I think Frost is so right to say, you don't have the prepared last line and then try to write a poem that will end there.

A. R. Ammons is a poet whose forms remain open and opportunistic, as is his philosophy, for that is the only way to approach the new nature which, the more we know about it in its shifting, provisional detail, the more we realize that we will never know it in any categorical way, because nature is more complex and elusive than any of our definitions of it:

> I see narrow orders, limited tightness, but will
> not run to that easy victory:
> still around the looser, wider forces work:
> I will try

to fasten into order enlarging grasps of disorder, widening
scope, but enjoying the freedom that
Scope eludes my grasp, that there is no finality of vision,
that I have perceived nothing completely,
that tomorrow a new walk is a new walk.

13

A personal history of reading

In the summer of 1957 it had been agreed that I was to do English at A level, and on the last day of term the English master called me to his desk in the fifth-form classroom and handed over a slim, dark-blue book. I was to read it during the summer. When I got back to my place I opened it – *Three Augustan Poets*, a selection of Gray, Collins and Cowper. I turned the pages, finding to my surprise that the poems I tried to read hardly made sense, as if they were written in some kind of code. But this did not matter in the intense excitement of the moment, which I perceived as a kind of rite of passage.

That August I went on the last of our family holidays, the last holiday of childhood, and I sealed the bargain I had made in the grammar school in Abergavenny by buying T. S. Eliot's *Selected Poems* at a bookshop in the resort. Again I had the experience of words not making sense – sitting reading *The Waste Land* on Bournemouth sands, I too could connect nothing with nothing, but this was combined again with excitement at the revelation that here was an entire world, a way of expression through language, about which I knew nothing, but about which I was going to learn. For much of that summer I just carried the books around with me, as if I could absorb their meaning through my palms. It was the beginning of a habit of systematic reading, which I have not been able to break in almost forty years.

Back at the grammar school I read Chaucer, Shakespeare, Dryden, the Augustan poets, Austen, Wordsworth, Forster and Lawrence for the A-level course. Outside that I remember getting involved in Dostoevsky, Kafka and Herman Hesse in translation, and being introduced to Dylan Thomas and R. S. Thomas. I took to the Thomases because of the way in which they used language and because they were Welsh, though my understanding of them (which must somehow have been in the air at school) was that they were Welsh tributaries to the great sea of English literature which I was studying – all literature in English, I somehow knew, contributed to that.[1]

This was a preparation, though I did not know it at the time, for my experience at university. I had applied for but failed to get a scholarship to Aberystwyth, and so I went to Birmingham instead. There we were expected to make an intensive study of every period, and most of the major writers, in English literature from the eighth century to the beginning of the twentieth. In my third year I had the option of reading twentieth-century literature or finishing the study of *Beowulf*. I chose *Beowulf*, partly because I was engrossed in the poem and partly because my Old English teacher, Geoffrey Shepherd, as I have since realized, had a brilliant scholarly mind. And anyway, I had already read many of the authors on the twentieth-century course.

What I studied in my three years as an undergraduate was the tradition of English literature as this had come to be formulated in British and American universities from around the 1920s on. It seemed at the time solid and unshakeable. and I could hardly know, graduating in 1963, that mine was almost the last generation of students to study English literature in this confident way.

My purpose-orientated habits of reading changed course when I did postgraduate work in medieval studies, for I shifted to history for my Ph.D. thesis on the social consequences of the Hundred Years War. With that in view I had to revive and extend my O-level Latin in order to read the medieval Latin of the fourteenth-century chroniclers, sermon writers and political satirists. And French to get at Anglo-Norman records and literature and the medieval French of Froissart and Christine de Pisan.

I had had no real cause to consider the European dimension to English culture before, except for the troublesome problem of

[1] A view to which, I learned later, R. S. Thomas appears to adhere (ambiguously) himself.

classical allusions which were nearly always cleared up in textbook footnotes. But now I began to realize the limited extent of my reading. As if on an archaeological site where there has been continuous settlement for many generations, I began digging down, and every layer as it was revealed added to and changed my understanding of what had come after. I realized that I could not fully understand what the fourteenth-century Latin chroniclers were up to if I did not understand their literary debt to the historians and rhetoricians of classical Rome. So I began reading Caesar, Tacitus and Livy, as well as those rhetorical treatises that were known in the fourteenth century and their medieval derivatives.

This course of reading was the result of curiosity and necessity, but I always had in mind the example of one great book, Ernst Robert Curtius's *European Literature and the Latin Middle Ages*, the scope of which is barely hinted at in its title. For the aim of Curtius was to demonstrate the continuity of European culture through dominant literary forms and ideas from Classical Greece and Rome, via an intermediary period of metamorphosis in the Latin Middle Ages, down to the modern era.

I read the book in my mid-twenties with awe. It sent me to reading classes in *The Divine Comedy* and *The Aeneid*, where we puzzled out the meaning of the poems line by line as I had done with *Beowulf* a few years before. But I never got far with either of them. The syntax of Classical Latin poetry was too difficult for me, and I secretly found Dante's picking over the torments of the damned distasteful. In the Dante reading class I never got beyond Hell. And I never worked down below the layers of Roman culture to the Greeks either, except to take a look at Aristotle's *The Art of Rhetoric* in translation.

By now I had read in these areas for ten years, but towards the end with an increasing sense of doggedness, of weariness, as if dragging my feet one after the other through sand. And around 1974 I gave up, turning away from the Classics and the Middle Ages to the twentieth century, to Modernist poetry and especially American poetry which I had hardly touched before. Eliot, Pound and Williams became the core of my reading, from which I radiated out to American poetry from the 1930s to the 1960s, as well as to English poetry of the period which, with the exception of Ted Hughes and one or two others, did not interest me as much.

This surfacing to modern times gave me an unexpected perspective on my reading of the previous fifteen years. In American universities at the beginning of the century, Pound and Eliot, I discovered, had been introduced to a similar idea of the great European tradition with living roots in Classical Antiquity, to which I had been drawn from reading Curtius. Pound's 'tradition', located firmly in the poetry of the troubadours, soon wobbled off into an eclectic mishmash that included Confucian philosophy and Chinese characters. But Eliot had remained loyal to the core idea – he made himself into the living embodiment of what Curtius meant by the European tradition.

Except that, from my perspective then, it seemed so artificial, such a deliberate act of the will. Curtius had published *European Literature and the Latin Middle Ages* in German in 1948. It is an extraordinary book, immensely learned, readable and persuasive in its plea for the historical unity of European culture in a living present after the catastrophe of two European-induced world wars. But it was at least two or more generations too late. That tradition had already crumbled when Eliot and Pound were undergraduates. In its place, British and American universities had hastily cobbled together a 'vernacular tradition' based on English literature with roots forged uneasily in Old English poetry. That too barely lasted thirty or forty years before being toppled in the wake of the campus revolt of 1968.

Pound saw most clearly when he wrote of the First World War in 'Hugh Selwyn Mauberley' that those who died in it had done so

> For an old bitch gone in the teeth,
> For a botched civilization . . .

And likewise Eliot in *The Waste Land*, when he made his protagonist look back at the end of the poem on an arid world, to reflect amid a clutch of macaronic quotations that, 'These fragments I have shored against my ruins'.

The whole Modernist European enterprise, as manifested in Eliot, did not work and could not work because, for this century, the great tradition of the European past no longer makes sense. It is not that it cannot be contemplated – there is a need to understand it as history. But as a tradition it is dead. It failed to survive as something vital and organic in the minds of people in our times, running out in the sands of the nineteenth century. The attempt to shore it up was wrong from the start. Eliot's great poem is *The Waste Land* not the Dantesque *Four Quartets*.

At about this time – the mid-1970s – I became curious about science, I think because the humanities in isolation seemed increasingly shallow. I was educated into a strong anti-science bias. This was never promoted overtly by my teachers so far as I recall, but was there implicitly in the fact that people studying the humanities in the fifties and sixties did not for the most part show the least curiosity about scientific discoveries and ideas. Science was shaping our world not merely through its application in technology but philosophically as well – and we ignored it.

Science was the antithesis of our world; its cold rationality (as we thought) was abhorrent; its impact on society (the Bomb) mostly for the worse. At the sixth form of the grammar school in Abergavenny, we divided quickly along the lines of our respective disciplines. Because the sixth form was small (I was the only one studying English in my year) science and humanities students mixed to some extent socially, but we never showed curiosity as to what the physics and chemistry students were up to. (Though nor, to be fair, did the science lot show curiosity about us – the lack of interest was mutual.)

Birmingham University in the sixties was a rapidly expanding institution with large, prestigious engineering departments. But in my eight years there I only met a science student or an engineer on a couple of occasions, when my prejudice that science had nothing to say to me was confirmed. Not that I ever discussed science at these times – I could not, because I did not know anything about it.

For myself, the roots of this prejudice – an ignorance brandished with pride – also fed off aspects of my personality and mental ability. From as far back as I can remember I have had an abhorrence of numbers. Contemplating even simple arithmetic gives me a sensation of nausea. I only passed the 11-plus exam because I was intensively coached in the maths paper by my schoolteacher and my mother. As soon as I squeaked through I wanted to forget what I had painfully learnt, only to be confronted by algebra and geometry, the most rudimentary principles of which I have never understood. I was withdrawn from the O-level maths exam because I got 0 in the mock.

I do not know why this should be so. I think my primary school teachers were at least adequate and I cannot recall any incident which could have triggered such an aversion. But whatever the cause, it was an insuperable disadvantage when it came to studying science.

This was compounded, however, by a purely personal quirk – my dislike of the laboratory where most lessons in chemistry and physics took place. I liked the jars of coloured chemicals that lined the walls, but I could not stand the smells of the place – the lingering stale smell of gas from the bunsen burners, and the overwhelming stinks of the gases released in some experiments, which made me want to retch. I cannot think where I got this fastidiousness from, but it was at one with my sense of the lab's ugliness, its barren reduction of everything to a kind of brutal utility. This, as least, is how it seems to me on reflection. At the time I merely absorbed a flow of negative sense impressions which almost inevitably I transferred to the subjects themselves.

But I was helped in this by the way physics and chemistry were taught. The method may have been good for boys who had an aptitude for science, but it was wrong for others like myself. I do not think we were introduced to any of the broader theories of science, or to the philosophy of science, which seem so interesting now, and which could easily be made understandable in outline to thirteen- and fourteen-year-olds. Everything was detail – beginning from the ground up, I suppose – from learning the valency table (what for?) to writing up trivial experiments (or so they seemed) in a grindingly dull language that was supposed to be objective (we were told) but which was death to the word. We must have been taught the simple structure of the atom, but I do not recall it, and I think this must be because it was presented so poorly, without excitement or imagination. As well as obnoxious to my finicky senses, I remember chemistry and physics lessons as monumentally dull.

The one exception in science was biology in which I did well and which was the only science subject I gained at O level. The biology lab was in a light and airy modern building on its own. It always had a clean smell, except sometimes for the whiff of formaldehyde which for some reason I did not mind. Biology was not a 'pure' science (I had internalized that prejudice even at school) but at least I understood it and could relate it to my world.

Then after O levels I forgot all this for more than twenty years, happy in prejudices which did not seem limiting to me at all. Until, that is, it was somehow borne in on me that this was a crippling flaw. How this happened, again I cannot be sure, but it was certainly related to a feeling in the mid-seventies that my reading had stalled – that no matter how widely or deeply I went on reading in the humanities, it would take me no further.

Related to this was an increasing frustration with the way in which the humanities were being treated in universities, where individual poems and novels were transformed into 'texts', and where primacy passed from the literature itself to the more and more arrogant pronouncements of literary theorists who jostled and back-stabbed for control of the syllabus. English departments in the seventies became as dull and spiritless as I remembered the chemistry lab at school, and in 1982 I quit.

By that time my programme of reading had already switched more or less to science, beginning with Isaac Asimov's two-volume *Guide to Science* which I wished that I had had at school, and progressing to popular books on chemistry, physics and astronomy. But innumeracy and my inability to think at any depth in abstract terms soon closed those areas off in all but the crudest terms.

Little by little my reading focused on biology in a return to what I had enjoyed the most at school. Biology too depends on mathematics but not in quite the same way or to the same degree as physics and chemistry, and I found I could get deeper into the subject. I like, too, the way that biology operates with the specific and the general but is rarely abstract in the sense that the pure sciences can seem to be. Finally I like the fact that it is a historical science, for this relates it to the inherently historical nature of the humanities. Evolutionary biology, which interests me most, is to me a logical extension of cultural history, for we cannot understand ourselves fully as cultural beings without understanding our history as a biological species. It is a realization which caused me to try to read in the areas of palaeo-anthropology and palaeontology in general, as well as evolutionary theory and related studies of our nearest relatives, the great apes.

A few years ago I visited Stevns Klint in Denmark which has become famous as one of the first sites where the iridium anomaly at the Cretaceous-Tertiary boundary was discovered, which led Walter and Luis Alvarez to posit an asteroid impact 65 million years ago as the main cause of the latest mass extinction to affect the Earth.[2]

At first I could not find the boundary in the creamy-white chalk and limestone cliff. And then there it was, an inch-thick line of soft reddish clay that rose gradually out of the base of the cliff along the inclined plane of the strata. I prized some out and placed my fingers in the hole, standing in cliff-shadow out of the heat, the Baltic lapping behind me. Over to the left in the distance were the trees and red roofs of Rødvig where the train would later take me back to Copenhagen and the power and assurance of our technology-driven civilization.

But here for a moment it was reduced to silence in the 65 million years packed into the rock that towered above me and the millions of years more that disappeared from view below the base of the cliff – the multiple realities of our time and deep time, that have to be shaped into a conformity if we are to understand what we are.

[2] See the essay 'Limits to imagination', ch. 2 above.

Afterthought

Two hercules swing low over the marsh then on to the
                                             estuary
right wings dipped like a salute
as they diminish in a drone round the headland

slow and determined,
the decision of the species to see things out
to the end.